The Wild Card

Other Books by Karl Shapiro

Person, Place, and Thing
V-Letter and Other Poems
Essay on Rime
Trial of a Poet
A Bibliography of Modern Prosody
Poems 1940–1953
Beyond Criticism (essays)
Poems of a Jew
American Poetry (editor)
In Defense of Ignorance (essays)
Start with the Sun (with James E. Miller Jr.
   and Bernice Slote)
The Bourgeois Poet
A Prosody Handbook (with Robert Beum)
Prose Keys to Modern Poetry (editor)
Selected Poems
Edsel (fiction)
To Abolish Children (essays)
White-Haired Lover
The Poetry Wreck (essays)
Adult Bookstore
Collected Poems 1940–1978
Love and War, Art and God
New and Selected Poems 1940–1986
The Younger Son (autobiography)
Reports of My Death (autobiography)
The Old Horsefly

Edited by Stanley Kunitz
and David Ignatow

Foreword by Stanley Kunitz

Introduction by M. L. Rosenthal

University of Illinois Press   Urbana and Chicago

Karl Shapiro

The Wild Card

**Selected Poems,
Early and Late**

PS
3537
.H27
A6
1998

Publication of this book was supported by a
grant from the Eric Mathieu King Fund of the
Academy of American Poets

Manufactured in the United States of America
1 2 3 4 5 C P 5 4 3 2 1

This book is printed on acid-free paper.

Typeset in 10/13 Janson by
Keystone Typesetting, Inc.

Library of Congress
Cataloging-in-Publication Data

Shapiro, Karl Jay, 1913–
The wild card : selected poems, early and late /
Karl Shapiro ; edited by Stanley Kunitz and
David Ignatow ; foreword by Stanley Kunitz ;
introduction by M.L. Rosenthal.
p. cm.
ISBN 0-252-02389-7 (alk. paper).
—ISBN 0-252-06689-8 (pbk. : alk. paper)
I. Kunitz, Stanley, 1905– . II. Ignatow, David,
1914– . III. Title.
PS3537.H27A6   1998
811'.52 —dc21   97-32579
CIP

To the memory of Susan Hanzo

— K.S.

Contents

From *Selected Poems*   (1968)

A Selection of Poems   (1969–92)

Foreword

Stanley Kunitz

The story of Karl Shapiro's famously brilliant literary debut, which generated more enthusiasm and acclaim than most poets experience in a lifetime, belongs to the annals of American poetry. In a memoir contributed to a festschrift for Shapiro's eightieth birthday, Hayden Carruth vividly recalls the impact of *Person, Place, and Thing* on an impressionable young college student in 1942: "I was excited by it in a way that I never had been before. . . . [I remember] how fresh, new, vigorous and pointed the poems were, how they awakened me to whole perspectives of poetic possibility that I had never suspected before. Here were poems taken from the American actuality I knew, from the technological world, cars, radios, industrial blight, the impersonality of death from machine . . . beautiful poems in a manner that I instantly recognized, the beauty of good, hard, varied metres and tough, functional rhymes" (in *Seriously Meeting Karl Shapiro*, ed. Sue Walker, 1993).

When Shapiro was awarded the Pulitzer Prize for his second collection of poems, *V-Letter* (1944), written and published while he was on military duty in the southwest Pacific, he seemed well on the way toward fulfilling Louise Bogan's prediction that "his work will become a sort of touchstone for his generation." But as his incisive introduction to the book pointedly indicated, Shapiro was in the process of evolving a quite different image of himself in his role as citizen poet:

> I have not written these poems to accord with any doctrine or system of thought or even a theory of composition. I have nothing to offer in the way of beliefs or challenges or prosody. I try to write freely, one day as a Christian, the next as a Jew, the next as a soldier who sees the gigantic slapstick of modern war. I hope I do not impersonate other poets. Certainly our contemporary man should feel divested of the stock attitudes of the last generation, the stance of the political intel-

lectual, the proletarian, the expert, the salesman, the world-traveler, the pundit-poet.

That self-analytical pronouncement anticipates the defiant litany of flamboyant paradoxes that would appear twenty years later in *The Bourgeois Poet*, beginning, "I am an atheist who says his prayers. I am an anarchist, and a full professor at that. I take the loyalty oath." Young as he was, Shapiro had an inkling that his destiny was to live as a free, quixotic, and iconoclastic spirit, a stormy presence in the house of letters. Savage wit, contradiction, and paradox would arm an imagination that had its roots in the lyric tradition. His voice would be the unappeasable voice of conscience.

Even his unprecedented appointment, at thirty-three, to the post of Consultant in Poetry to the Library of Congress (now termed Poet Laureate of the United States) did not divert him from his course or induce him to modify the blazing candor that drove his art. He was not tamed by prizes and honors or inclined by temperament to play it safe by writing predictably perfect sestinas on innocuous themes. For reasons that pertain to the life as well as to the work, Carruth acknowledges his debt and that of his generation to the bold example set by "Shapiro's poetic courage, his willingness to change, his insistence on it."

When *The Bourgeois Poet* appeared in 1964, critics who had lauded Shapiro's mastery of craft were among those who felt challenged by his dismissal of meter and rhyme as nonessential and artificial impediments to the poetic process. "All things remain to be simplified," he wrote. "I must break free of the poetry trap." A surprising number of fellow-poets were not amused by his obituary quip on the current state of the art: "I didn't go to the funeral of poetry. I stayed home and watched it on television." Satiric, erotic, outrageous, apocalyptic, *The Bourgeois Poet* is simultaneously a book of self-revelation, a poet's zigzag manifesto, and a cry of the heart against the ills of an age. Yes, this was a work for which he paid dearly, but it was worth the cost, and it remains triumphant.

"What would American poetry be like, to deserve the name?" Shapiro has asked; and he has replied, with a nod to Walt Whitman, "It would be nonsensical, hilarious, and obscene like us. Absurd like us." All American poetry, he contends, tries to measure up to *Leaves of Grass*. His own poem in homage to Whitman is small in scale, but its grand and, indeed, "hilarious" finale exemplifies the relaxed style, vernacular tone, and esprit of the best of his later, mostly neglected verse:

Two hundred pounds of genius and hype,
Nature-mystic who designed his tomb

Solid as an Egyptian pyramid,
American to the soles of his boots,
Outspoken as Christ or Madame Blavatsky,
Messiah, Muse of the Modern, Mother!

There are times when the risks that Shapiro takes in the course of his poems seem on the verge of becoming unmanageable, but he has a way of overriding difficulties through the sheer momentum of his creative energy. In a game where aces are wild he has a gambler's faith that luck is on the side of those who dare.

As we prepare to go to press, my thoughts turn to my friend, the late David Ignatow, whose distinctive contribution to this undertaking is recognized on the title page. In his last communication with me, he remarked, "I must tell you how good I feel about helping to pass these poems on, so that they can be discovered again. Isn't that part of our obligation?"

Karl's own words would seem to indicate that this is a propitious time for publication. As far back as 1975, in the foreword to his selected essays *The Poetry Wreck*, he speculated that on the arrival of the millennium — now so near at hand — there will be a day of judgment for the poets of this century. "Strip away from twentieth-century poetry all the sociology and all the politics and see what is left," he wrote. "Precious little, perhaps, but something to conjure with, something our descendants will remember us by."

Here is *The Wild Card*, definitely something to conjure with.

Introduction:
"Shapiro Is All Right!"

M. L. Rosenthal

"Shapiro Is All Right!" Thus exclaimed the title of a review, years ago, of one of Karl Shapiro's books in the *New York Times Book Review*. The reviewer was William Carlos Williams, Shapiro's senior by three decades and our best-loved avant-garde model since the late 1920s. It was a bit of a surprise. The inventor of the "variable foot," experimenter *par excellence* in search of a poetry rooted in American idiom and speech-rhythms, was praising Shapiro, who had gained his early fame working in conventional forms, with debts to Auden and other British figures. The present collection shows why the younger poet won the Old Master's shout of approval.

Shapiro's rapid leap into recognition, marked by a Pulitzer award, the poetry consultantship at the Library of Congress, the editorship of *Poetry: A Magazine of Verse*, and university professorships, had seemed to take him far from Williams's embattled world. But if we look back at the pieces in his early collection *Person, Place, and Thing* (1942), we can see implicit affinities — continuities of attitude and sensibility from the two preceding decades — after all.

The particular American historical moment, in the immediate wake of the relatively Left-tending, socially critical Depression era, was also one of mobilization against the Axis powers and their ideology. Shapiro himself, serving with the army in the South Pacific when his book came out, was hardly a gung-ho flagwaver. His poem "Conscription Camp," set in Virginia, swings a double saber-slash of disgust against both the South's history and any sort of glib patriotism:

> You manufacture history like jute —
> Labor is cheap, Virginia, for high deeds,
> But in your British dream of reputation
> The black man is your conscience and your cost.
> . . . .

The sunrise gun rasps in the throat of heaven;
The lungs of dawn are heavy and corrupt;
We hawk and spit; our flag walks through the air
Breathing hysteria thickly in each face.

Other pieces in *Person, Place, and Thing* reveal an anarcho-bohemian edge akin to Williams's but more emphatic in their antiracist and radical sympathies: attitudes that many young American Jews of Shapiro's generation shared with him. (The amusing, self-ironic sixth poem of his autobiographical sequence "Recapitulations," in his 1947 volume *Trial of a Poet*, describes his younger days when, as he has written, he "raved like a scarlet banner.") He had attended the University of Virginia, and his poem "University" begins, memorably: "To hurt the Negro and avoid the Jew / Is the curriculum."

Another early poem, "Death of Emma Goldman," described that passionate anarchist, "dark conscience of the family" (her own and humanity's), with gentle appreciation. At the same time, it reviled the people who, after her death, called her immoral because she never married her lover, Alexander Berkman:

Triumphant at the final breath,
        Their senile God, their cops,
All the authorities and friends pro tem
Passing her pillow, keeping her concerned.
But the cowardly obit was already written:
Morning would know she was a common slut.

Given the general ignorance, including that of most intellectuals, about Emma Goldman or anarchism, such poetry was hardly what won Shapiro his first success. Other reasons were far more compelling. For one thing, he was our first young American to emerge as a serious poet of World War II. For another, he had the splendid knack of being able to project a heightened vision of commonplace objects and circumstances. Many of his "civilian" poems are brilliant closeups of this sort. One example is "The Dome of Sunday," which points its lens — perhaps unfairly but "with focus sharp as Flemish-painted face / In film of varnish brightly fixed" — on the poet's prosperous Baltimore neighbors as hopelessly vulgar and self-centered. Others include "Buick," a witty, sexy, very American love song to a car, and the swift-moving, terrified "Auto Wreck." In the military context, the candidly gloomy picture of young, newly enlisted soldiers (including the poet) in "Conscription Camp" is similarly precise and evocative:

Through the long school of day, absent in heart,
Distant in every thought but self we tread,
Wheeling in blocks like large expensive toys
That never understand except through fun.

To steal aside as aimlessly as curs
Is our desire; to stare at corporals
As sceptically as boys; not to believe
The misty-eyed letter and the cheap snapshot.

Shapiro's first volume showed he could also write lyrical pieces whose feeling, despite their subtleties, had the direct appeal of folksongs. This gift has been a winning wild card for him, from the beginning to the more recent poems at the close of this collection. One moving early instance, expressing the pang of separation from home and from one's beloved in wartime, is his poem "Nostalgia." It begins:

My soul stands at the window of my room,
    And I ten thousand miles away;
My days are filled with Ocean's sound of doom,
    Salt and cloud and the bitter spray.
Let the wind blow, for many a man shall die.

My selfish youth, my books with gilded edge,
    Knowledge and all gaze down the street;
The potted plants along the window ledge
    Gaze down with selfish lives and sweet.
Let the wind blow, for many a man shall die.

My night is now her day, my day her night,
    So I lie down, and so I rise;
The sun burns close, the star is losing height,
    The clock is hunted down the skies.
Let the wind blow, for many a man shall die.

Not to labor the point, the music of pure lyricism makes a number of Shapiro's poems unforgettable, whether in a psychologically demanding piece like "The Figurehead" (about coping with a paralytic friend's "cold torture" as he lies imprisoned "on the treacherous shoals of his bed"); or in a piercing war poem like "Full Moon: New Guinea" (a Shakespearean sonnet about waiting in fear for the bombers to strike on a beautiful moonlit night); or in a tender, troubled gesture of understanding like "Mongolian Idiot."

Shapiro's celebration of the inevitable contradictions in our moral natures, his cultivation of what we might call a principled ambivalence, reaches its climax in his 1964 sequence *The Bourgeois Poet*. It is there, too, that Shapiro, a genuine virtuoso of conventional metrics, repudiates what he calls "the cosmetology of font and rule, meters laid on like fingernail enamel." "Why," he asks —

> Why the attractive packaging of stanza? Those cartons so pretty, shall I open them up? Why the un-American activity of the sonnet? Why must grown people listen to rhyme? How much longer the polite applause, the tickle in the throat?

The Bourgeois Poet, made up mainly of prose poems, provides the fullest example of Shapiro's shifted poetic values. To some extent it is a series of notebook entries whose essential rhythm is a kind of oracular musing that can rise to a lyrical pitch. Baudelaire may well be the major model for Shapiro in this form. But at times we hear reminiscences of a whole range of free inventors from Whitman through Williams, Fearing, and the Beats. The sound-patterns — shorter units, many single lines, and chantlike parallelism — echo them, and so does the recurrent mockery of fixed attitudes. But Shapiro's idiosyncratic humor and phrasing — and, even more, his introspective obsession with the ambivalence and unresolvable terror life forces upon us — keep the ultimate effect underivatively his own. Thus, section 34 in the original text begins in a series of laughingly depreciative and paradoxical self-definitions:

> I am an atheist who says his prayers.

> I am an anarchist, and a full professor at that. I take the loyalty oath.

> I am a deviate. I fondle and contribute, backscuttle and brown, father of three.

But later it opens itself to more mordant, fear-ridden utterances:

> My century, take savagery to your heart. Take wooden
>   idols, walk them through the streets. Bow down to Science.

> My century that boils history to a pulp for newspaper, my century of
>   the million-dollar portrait, century of the decipherment of
>   Linear B and the old scrolls, century of the dream of penultimate
>   man (he wanders among the abandoned skyscrapers of Kansas;
>   he has already forgotten language), century of the turning-point
>   of time, the human wolf pack and the killing light.

To re-read Shapiro's work in the unfolding, expanding scroll of his entire career is to see its manysidedness as never before. His is the essential, relentlessly self-scrutinizing modern Jewish sensibility. He was hard on his own people in "The Dome of Sunday" and yet expressed in "Israel" his giddy joy at the founding of the Jewish state — *and yet*, for the most part, shares the secular, antidogmatic mentality that permeates the leading thought of our era, when, indeed, "The best lack all conviction, while the worst / Are full of passionate intensity." (The lines are of course Yeats's, whom Shapiro once parodied, cleverly and affectionately, in his poem "Going to School." What they imply is very much what Shapiro meant in the passage about "my century" quoted in the preceding paragraph.)

And more intimately, he is also a poet who deals with desolation as well as joy in love and marriage, and who would be as toughminded as he often claims to be if only his humanity did not stand in the way. He may have begun his exuberantly ugly poem "The Fly" with the apostrophe "O hideous little bat, the size of snot." But that masterpiece of revulsion is at least counterbalanced by the concluding sonnet of a little group called "The Interlude," which in its way sums up the pathetic contradictions poets must confront and perhaps, if possible, even resolve:

> Writing, I crushed an insect with my nail
> And thought nothing at all. A bit of wing
> Caught my eye then, a gossamer so frail
>
> And exquisite, I saw in it a thing
> That scorned the grossness of the thing I wrote.
> It hung upon my finger like a sting.
>
> A leg I noticed next, fine as a mote,
> "And on this frail eyelash he walked," I said,
> "And climbed and walked like any mountain-goat."
>
> And in this mood I sought the little head,
> But it was lost; then in my heart a fear
> Cried out, "A life — why beautiful, why dead!"
>
> It was a mite that held itself most dear,
> So small I could have drowned it with a tear.

From
Person, Place, and Thing
(1942)

The Dome of Sunday

With focus sharp as Flemish-painted face
In film of varnish brightly fixed
And through a polished hand-lens deeply seen,
Sunday at noon through hyaline thin air
Sees down the street,
And in the camera of my eye depicts
Row-houses and row-lives:
Glass after glass, door after door the same.
Face after face the same, the same,
The brutal visibility the same;

As if one life emerging from one house
Would pause, a single image caught between
Two facing mirrors where vision multiplies
Beyond perspective,
A silent clatter in the high-speed eye
Spinning out photo-circulars of sight.

I see slip to the curb the long machines
Out of whose warm and windowed rooms pirouette
Shellacked with silk and light
The hard legs of our women.
Our women are one woman, dressed in black.
The carmine printed mouth
And cheeks as soft as muslin-glass belong
Outright to one dark dressy man,
Merely a swagger at her curvy side.
This is their visit to themselves:
All day from porch to porch they weave
A nonsense pattern through the even glare,
Stealing in surfaces
Cold vulgar glances at themselves.

And high up in the heated room all day
I wait behind the plate glass pane for one,
Hot as a voyeur for a glimpse of one,
The vision to blot out this woman's sheen;
All day my sight records expensively
Row-houses and row-lives.

But nothing happens; no diagonal
With melting shadow falls across the curb:
Neither the blinded negress lurching through fatigue,
Nor exiles bleeding from their pores,
Nor that bright bomb slipped lightly from its rack
To splinter every silvered glass and crystal prism,
Witch-bowl and perfume bottle
And billion candle-power dressing-bulb,
No direct hit to smash the shatter-proof
And lodge at last the quivering needle
Clean in the eye of one who stands transfixed
In fascination of her brightness.

Washington Cathedral

From summer and the wheel-shaped city
That sweats like a swamp and wrangles on
Its melting streets, white mammoth Forums,
And political hotels with awnings, caryatids;
Past barricaded embassies with trees
That shed trash and parch his eyes,
To here, the acres of superior quiet,
Shadow and damp, the tourist comes,
And, cooled by stones and darkness, stares.

Tall as a lover's night, the nave
Broods over him, irradiates,
And stars of color out of painted glass
Shoot downward on apostles and on chairs
Huddled by hundreds under altar rails.
Yet it is only Thursday; there are no prayers,

But exclamations. The lady invokes by name
The thousand-odd small sculptures, spooks,
New angels, pitted roods; she gives
The inventory of relics to his heart
That aches with history and astonishment:
He gives a large coin to a wooden coffer.

Outside, noon blazes in his face like guns.
He goes down by the Bishop's walk, the dial,
The expensive grass, the Byzantine bench,
While stark behind him a red naked crane
Hangs over the unfinished transept,
A Cubist hen rivalling the Gothic School.

Whether he sees the joke; whether he cares;
Whether he tempts a vulgar miracle,
Some deus ex machina, this is his choice,
A shrine of whispers and tricky penumbras.
	Therefore he votes again for the paid
Clergy, the English hint, the bones of Wilson
Crushed under tons of fake magnificence.
	Nor from the zoo of his instincts
	Come better than crude eagles: now
He cannot doubt that violent obelisk
And Lincoln whittled to a fool's colossus.
This church and city triumph in his eyes.
He is only a good alien, nominally happy.

Auto Wreck

Its quick soft silver bell beating, beating,
And down the dark one ruby flare
Pulsing out red light like an artery.
The ambulance at top speed floating down
Past beacons and illuminated clocks
Wings in a heavy curve, dips down,
And brakes speed, entering the crowd.
The doors leap open, emptying light;
Stretchers are laid out, the mangled lifted
And stowed into the little hospital.
Then the bell, breaking the hush, tolls once,
And the ambulance with its terrible cargo
Rocking, slightly rocking, moves away,
As the doors, an afterthought, are closed.

We are deranged, walking among the cops
Who sweep glass and are large and composed.
One is still making notes under the light.
One with a bucket douches ponds of blood
Into the street and gutter.
One hangs lanterns on the wrecks that cling,
Empty husks of locusts, to iron poles.

Our throats were tight as tourniquets,
Our feet were bound with splints, but now,
Like convalescents intimate and gauche,
We speak through sickly smiles and warn
With the stubborn saw of common sense,
The grim joke and the banal resolution.
The traffic moves around with care,
But we remain, touching a wound
That opens to our richest horror.
Already old, the question Who shall die?
Becomes unspoken Who is innocent?

For death in war is done by hands;
Suicide has cause and stillbirth, logic;
And cancer, simple as a flower, blooms.
But this invites the occult mind,
Cancels our physics with a sneer,
And spatters all we knew of denouement
Across the expedient and wicked stones.

Hospital

Inside or out, the key is pain. It holds
The florist to your pink medicinal rose,
The nickname to the corpse. One wipes it from
Blue German blades or drops it down the drain;
The novelist with a red tube up his nose
Gingerly pets it. Nurse can turn it off.

This is the Oxford of all sicknesses.
Kings have lain here and fabulous small Jews
And actresses whose legs were always news.
In this black room the painter lost his sight,
The crippled dancer here put down her shoes,
And the scholar's memory broke, like an old clock.

These reached to heaven and inclined their heads
While starchy angels reached them into beds:
These stooped to hell to labor out their time,
Or choked to death in seas of glaucous slime:
All tasted fire, and then, their hate annealed,
Ate sad ice-cream and wept upon a child.

What church is this, what factory of souls
Makes the bad good and fashions a new nose,
And the doctors reel with Latin and even the dead
Expect the unexpected? For O the souls
Fly back like heavy homing-birds to roost
In long-racked limbs, filling the lonely boughs.

The dead cry *life* and stagger up the hill;
But is there still the incorrigible city where
The well enjoy their poverty and the young
Worship the gutter? Is Wednesday still alive
And Tuesday wanting terribly to sin?
Hush, there are many pressing the oak doors,

Saying, "Are boys and girls important fears?
Can you predict the elections by my guts?"
But the rubber gloves are deep in a deep wound,
Stitching a single heart. These far surpass
Themselves, their wives, and the removed goiter;
Are, for the most part, human but unbandaged.

The Fly

O hideous little bat, the size of snot,
With polyhedral eye and shabby clothes,
To populate the stinking cat you walk
The promontory of the dead man's nose,
Climb with the fine leg of a Duncan-Phyfe
 The smoking mountains of my food
  And in a comic mood
 In mid-air take to bed a wife.

Riding and riding with your filth of hair
On gluey foot or wing, forever coy,
Hot from the compost and green sweet decay,
Sounding your buzzer like an urchin toy —
You dot all whiteness with diminutive stool,
 In the tight belly of the dead
  Burrow with hungry head
 And inlay maggots like a jewel.

At your approach the great horse stomps and paws
Bringing the hurricane of his heavy tail;
Shod in disease you dare to kiss my hand
Which sweeps against you like an angry flail;
Still you return, return, trusting your wing
 To draw you from the hunter's reach
  That learns to kill to teach
 Disorder to the tinier thing.

My peace is your disaster. For your death
Children like spiders cup their pretty hands
And wives resort to chemistry of war.
In fens of sticky paper and quicksands
You glue yourself to death. Where you are stuck
 You struggle hideously and beg,
  You amputate your leg
 Imbedded in the amber muck.

But I, a man, must swat you with my hate,
Slap you across the air and crush your flight,
Must mangle with my shoe and smear your blood,
Expose your little guts pasty and white,
Knock your head sidewise like a drunkard's hat.
    Pin your wings under like a crow's,
        Tear off your flimsy clothes
    And beat you as one beats a rat.

Then like Gargantua I stride among
The corpses strewn like raisins in the dust,
The broken bodies of the narrow dead
That catch the throat with fingers of disgust.
I sweep. One gyrates like a top and falls
    And stunned, stone blind, and deaf
        Buzzes its frightful F
    And dies between three cannibals.

University

To hurt the Negro and avoid the Jew
Is the curriculum. In mid-September
The entering boys, identified by hats,
Wander in a maze of mannered brick
    Where boxwood and magnolia brood
    And columns with imperious stance
    Like rows of ante-bellum girls
        Eye them, outlanders.

In whited cells, on laws equipped for peace,
Under the arch, and lofty banister,
Equals shake hands, unequals blankly pass;
The exemplary weather whispers, "Quiet, quiet"
    And visitors on tiptoe leave
    For the raw North, the unfinished West,
    As the young, detecting an advantage,
        Practice a face.

Where, on their separate hill, the colleges,
Like manor houses of an older law,
Gaze down embankments on a land in fee,
The Deans, dry spinsters over family plate,
    Ring out the English name like coin,
    Humor the snob and lure the lout.
    Within the precincts of this world
        Poise is a club.

But on the neighboring range, misty and high,
The past is absolute: some luckless race
Dull with inbreeding and conformity
Wears out its heart, and comes barefoot and bad
    For charity or jail. The scholar
    Sanctions their obsolete disease;
    The gentleman revolts with shame
        At his ancestor.

And the true nobleman, once a democrat,
Sleeps on his private mountain. He was one
Whose thought was shapely and whose dream was broad;
This school he held his art and epitaph.
    But now it takes from him his name,
    Falls open like a dishonest look,
    And shows us, rotted and endowed,
        Its senile pleasure.

Drug Store

I do remember an apothecary,
And hereabouts 'a dwells

It baffles the foreigner like an idiom,
And he is right to adopt it as a form
Less serious than the living-room or bar;
      For it disestablishes the café,
Is a collective, and on basic country.

Not that it praises hygiene and corrupts
The ice-cream parlor and the tobacconist's
Is it a center; but that the attractive symbols
      Watch over puberty and leer
Like rubber bottles waiting for sick-use.

Youth comes to jingle nickels and crack wise;
The baseball scores are his, the magazines
Devoted to lust, the jazz, the Coca-Cola,
      The lending-library of love's latest.
He is the customer; he is heroized.

And every nook and cranny of the flesh
Is spoken to by packages with wiles.
"Buy me, buy me," they whimper and cajole;
      The hectic range of lipsticks pouts,
Revealing the wicked and the simple mouth.

With scarcely any evasion in their eye
They smoke, undress their girls, exact a stance;
But only for a moment. The clock goes round;
      Crude fellowships are made and lost;
They slump in booths like rags, not even drunk.

Haircut

O wonderful nonsense of lotions of Lucky Tiger,
Of savory soaps and oils of bottle-bright green,
The gold of liqueurs, the unguents of Newark and Niger,
Powders and balms and waters washing me clean;

In mirrors of marble and silver I see us forever
Increasing, decreasing the puzzles of luminous spaces
As I turn, am revolved and am pumped in the air on a lever,
With the backs of my heads in chorus with all of my faces.

Scissors and comb are mowing my hair into neatness,
Now pruning my ears, now smoothing my neck like a plain;
In the harvest of hair and the chaff of powdery sweetness
My snow-covered slopes grow dark with the wooly rain.

And the little boy cries, for it hurts to sever the curl,
And we too are quietly bleating to part with our coat.
Does the barber want blood in a dish? I am weak as a girl,
I desire my pendants, the fatherly chin of a goat.

I desire the pants of a bear, the nap of a monkey
Which trousers of friction have blighted down to my skin.
I am bare as a tusk, as jacketed up as a flunkey,
With the chest of a moth-eaten camel growing within.

But in death we shall flourish, you summer-dark leaves of my head,
While the flesh of the jaw ebbs away from the shores of my teeth;
You shall cover my sockets and soften the boards of my bed
And lie on the flat of my temples as proud as a wreath.

Waitress

Whoever with the compasses of his eyes
Is plotting the voyage of your steady shape
As you come laden through the room and back
And rounding your even bottom like a Cape
Crooks his first finger, whistles through his lip
Till you arrive, all motion, like a ship,

He is my friend — consider his dark pangs
And love of Niger, naked indigence,
Dance him the menu of a poem and squirm
Deep in the juke-box jungle, green and dense.
Surely he files his teeth, punctures his nose,
Carves out the god and takes off all his clothes.

For once, the token on the table's edge
Sufficing, proudly and with hair unpinned
You mounted the blueplate, stretched out and grinned
Like Christmas fish and turkey pink and skinned,
Eyes on the half-shell, loin with parsley stuck,
Thigh-bones and ribs and little toes to suck.

I speak to you, ports of the northern myth,
This dame is carved and eaten. One by one,
God knows what hour, her different parts go home,
Lastly her pants, and day or night is done;
But on the restaurant the sign of fear
Reddens and blazes — "English spoken here."

Buick

As a sloop with a sweep of immaculate wing on her delicate spine
And a keel as steel as a root that holds in the sea as she leans,
Leaning and laughing, my warm-hearted beauty, you ride, you ride,
You tack on the curves with parabola speed and a kiss of goodbye,
Like a thoroughbred sloop, my new high-spirited spirit, my kiss.

As my foot suggests that you leap in the air with your hips of a girl,
My finger that praises your wheel and announces your voices of song,
Flouncing your skirts, you blueness of joy, you flirt of politeness,
You leap, you intelligence, essence of wheelness with silvery nose,
And your platinum clocks of excitement stir like the hairs of a fern.

But how alien you are from the booming belts of your birth and the smoke
Where you turned on the stinging lathes of Detroit and Lansing at night
And shrieked at the torch in your secret parts and the amorous tests,
But now with your eyes that enter the future of roads you forget;
You are all instinct with your phosphorous glow and your streaking hair.

And now when we stop it is not as the bird from the shell that I leave
Or the leathery pilot who steps from his bird with a sneer of delight,
And not as the ignorant beast do you squat and watch me depart,
But with exquisite breathing you smile, with satisfaction of love,
And I touch you again as you tick in the silence and settle in sleep.

Israfel

la tombe de Poe éblouissante

Picture the grave in his diabolical dream
Where death would come with clues and scenery,
The bulbous forehead and the crooked mouth
Leaking a poison, the translucent hands.

Perhaps like Juliet he could come alive
To hate Longfellow and to outrage life,
But dare not from his wretched rusty stone,
Landmark for girls developing in slums.

Here he is local color, another crank;
Pawnshops and whores and sour little bars
Accept him. Neither alarming nor prophetic,
He pleases like a wop or a jack-o-lantern.

Others uptown forgive his nasty eyes
Because he was sick and had a mind to err;
But he was never dirty like Hawthorne,
But boyish with his spooks and funerals

And clammy virgins. What else were his codes
But diagrams of hideouts of the mind
Plugged up with corpses and expensive junk,
Prosopopoeia to keep himself at bay?

Think of him as a cicerone with data
False as a waxworks and that understood
Ask pitifully for pain. Or think that now
Four cities claim him as France recommended.

Mongolian Idiot

A dog that spoke, a monster born of sheep
We mercilessly kill, and kill the thought,
Yet house the parrot and let the centaur go,
These being to their nature and those not.
We laugh at apes, that never quite succeed
       At eating soup or wearing hats.

Adam had named so many but not this,
This that would name a curse when it had come,
Unfinished man, or witch, or myth, or sin,
Not ever father and never quite a son.
Ape had outstripped him, dog and darling lamb
       And all the kindergarten beasts.

Enter the bare room of his mind and count
His store of words with letters large and black;
See how he handles clumsily those blocks
With swans and sums; his colored picture books.
At thirty-five he squeals to see the ball
       Bounce in the air and roll away.

Pity and fear we give this innocent
Who maimed his mother's beautiful instinct;
But she would say, "My body had a dog;
I bore the ape and nursed the crying sheep.
He is my kindness and my splendid gift
       Come from all life and for all life."

Necropolis

Even in death they prosper; even in the death
Where lust lies senseless and pride fallow
The mouldering owners of rents and labor
Prosper and improve the high hill.

For theirs is the stone whose name is deepest cut,
Theirs the facsimile temple, theirs
The iron acanthus and the hackneyed Latin,
The boxwood rows and all the birds.

And even in death the poor are thickly herded
In intimate congestion under streets and alleys.
Look at the standard sculpture, the cheap
Synonymous slabs, the machined crosses.

Yes, even in death the cities are unplanned.
The heirs govern from the old centers;
They will not remove. And the ludicrous angels,
Remains of the poor, will never fly
But only multiply in the green grass.

October 1

That season when the leaf deserts the bole
And half-dead see-saws through the October air
Falling face-downward on the walks to print
The decalcomania of its little soul —
Hardly has the milkman's sleepy horse
On wooden shoes echoed across the blocks,
When with its back jaws open like a dredge
The van comes lumbering up the curb to someone's door and knocks.

And four black genii muscular and shy
Holding their shy caps enter the first room
Where someone hurriedly surrenders up
The thickset chair, the mirror half awry,
Then to their burdens stoop without a sound.
One with his bare hands rends apart the bed,
One stuffs the china-barrel with stale print,
Two bear the sofa toward the door with dark funereal tread.

The corner lamp, the safety eye of night,
Enveloped in the sun blinks and goes blind
And soon the early risers pick their way
Through kitchenware and pillows bolt upright.
The bureau on the sidewalk with bare back
And wrinkling veneer is most disgraced,
The sketch of Paris suffers in the wind,
Only the bike, its nose against the wall, does not show haste.

Two hours — the movers mop their necks and look,
Filing through dust and echoes back and forth.
The halls are hollow and all the floors are cleared
Bare to the last board, to the most secret nook;
But on the street a small chaos survives
That slowly now the leviathan ingests,
And schoolboys and stenographers stare at
The truck, the house, the husband in his hat who stands and rests.

He turns with miserable expectant face
And for the last time enters. On the wall
A picture-stain spreads from the nail-hole down.
Each object live and dead has left its trace.
He leaves his key; but as he quickly goes
This question comes behind: Did someone die?
Is someone rich or poor, better or worse?
What shall uproot a house and bring this care into his eye?

Epitaph for John and Richard

There goes the clock; there goes the sun;
Greenwich is right with Arlington;
The signal's minutes are signifying
That somebody old has finished dying,
That somebody young has just begun.

What do you think you earned today
Except the waste, except the pay,
Except the power to be spending?
And now your year is striking, ending,
What do you think you have put away?

Only a promise, only a life
Squandered in secret with a wife
In bedtime feigning and unfeigning;
The blood has long since ceased complaining;
The clock has satisfied the strife.

They will not cast your honored head
Or say from lecterns what you said,
But only keep you with them all
Committed in the City Hall;
Once born, once married, and once dead.

Emporium

He must have read Aladdin who rubbed his head
And brought this out of space; some genie came
With bolts of lawn and rugs of heavy red,
Shoes for white boxes, gems for velvet trays;
For who could authorize in his right name
Such pricelessness of time and recklessness of days?

Not Faust, who longed for Hell, would sell his light
For moving stairs and mirrors set in miles
Where wives might wander with their sex in sight;
Rage and rat's-logic this man must have known
Who built these buttresses on rotted piles,
Initialed every brick, and carved his lips in stone.

As if the ancient principle obtained
And solvent time would underwrite his debt,
Or the strong face of flesh were not profaned
For mannikins with hair of cloth-of-gold;
As if no tongue had ever questioned yet
Who buys and who is bought, who sells and who is sold.

But those politely dressed in normal drab
Shall think of him remotely, think with shame
How of their skill, their goodness and their gab
He trained his joys to be obsequious Jews;
At last not even wives shall goad his name
To feats of wealth, humility, and sickness-news;

So that, with rounded ruins honored, like Stonehenge,
Time shall have time, and he his impotent revenge.

Death of Emma Goldman

Triumphant of the final breath,
    Their senile God, their cops,
All the authorities and friends pro tem
Passing her pillow, keeping her concerned.
But the cowardly obit was already written:
Morning would know she was a common slut.

    Russians who stood for tragedy
        Were sisters all around;
Dark conscience of the family, down she lay
To end the career of passion, brain a bruise;
And mother-wonder filled her like a tide,
Rabid and raging discipline to bear.

    In came the monarchist, a nurse,
        And covered up her eyes;
Volkstaat of hate took over: suddenly
The Ego gagged, the Conscious overpowered,
The Memory beaten to a pulp, she fell.
It remained to hide the body, or make it laugh.

    Yet not to sink her name in coin
        Like Caesar was her wish,
To come alive like Frick, conjecture maps,
Or speak with kings of low mentality,
But to be left alone, a law to scorn
Of all, and none more honored than the least.

    This way she died, though premature
        Her clarity for others;
For it was taught that, listening, the soul
Lost track and merged with trespasses and spies
Whose black renown shook money like a rat
And showed up grass a mortmain property.

The Contraband

I dreamed I held a poem and knew
The capture of a living thing.
Boys in a Grecian circle sang
And women at their harvesting.

Slowly I tried to wake and draw
The vision after, word by word,
But sleep was covetous: the song
The singers and the singing blurred.

The paper flowers of everynight
All die. Day has no counterpart,
Where memory writes its boldface wish
And swiftly punishes the heart.

Elegy for Two Banjos

Haul up the flag, you mourners,
      Not half-mast but all the way;
The funeral is done and disbanded;
      The devil's had the final say.

O mistress and wife too pensive,
      Pallbearers and priestly men,
Put your black clothes in the attic,
      And get up on your feet again.

Death did his job like a scholar,
      A most unusual case,
Death did his job like a gentleman;
      He barely disturbed the face.

You packed him in a handsome carton,
      Set the lid with silver screws;
You dug a dark pit in the graveyard
      To tell the white worms the news.

Now you've nothing left to remember,
      Nothing but the words he wrote,
But they'll never let you remember,
      Only stick like a bone in your throat.

O if I'd been his wife or mistress,
      His pallbearer or his parish priest,
I'd have kept him at home forever —
      Or as long as bric-a-brac at least.

I would have burned his body
      And salvaged a sizable bone
For a paper-weight or a door-stop
      Or a garden flagstone.

I would have heaped the fire
       And boiled his beautiful skull.
It was laden like a ship for travels
       And now is but an empty hull.

I would have dried it off in linens,
       Polished it with a chamois cloth
Till it shone like a brand-new quarter
       And felt smooth as the nose of a moth.

Or I'd have hung it out in the garden
       Where everything else is alive,
Put a queen bee in the brain case
       So the bees could build a hive.

Maybe I'd have wired the jawbone
       With a silver spring beneath,
Set it in the cradle with baby
       So baby could rattle the teeth.

O you didn't do right by William
       To shove him down that filthy hole,
Throw him a lot of tears and Latin
       And a cheap "God bless your soul."

You might as well leave off mourning,
       His photograph is getting dim,
So you'd better take a long look at it
       For it's all you'll ever see of him.

Haul up the flag, you mourners,
       Not half-mast but all the way;
The funeral is done and disbanded;
       The devil's had the final say.

Scyros

snuffle and sniff and handkerchief

The doctor punched my vein
The captain called me Cain
Upon my belly sat the sow of fear
With coins on either eye
The President came by
And whispered to the braid what none could hear

High over where the storm
Stood steadfast cruciform
The golden eagle sank in wounded wheels
White Negroes laughing still
Crept fiercely on Brazil
Turning the navies upward on their keels

Now one by one the trees
Stripped to their naked knees
To dance upon the heaps of shrunken dead
The roof of England fell
Great Paris tolled her bell
And China staunched her milk and wept for bread

No island singly lay
But lost its name that day
The Ainu dived across the plunging sands
From dawn to dawn to dawn
King George's birds came on
Strafing the tulips from his children's hands

Thus in the classic sea
Southeast from Thessaly
The dynamited mermen washed ashore
And tritons dressed in steel
Trolled heads with rod and reel
And dredged potatoes from the Aegean floor

Hot is the sky and green
Where Germans have been seen
The moon leaks metal on the Atlantic fields
Pink boys in birthday shrouds
Loop lightly through the clouds
Or coast the peaks of Finland on their shields

That prophet year by year
Lay still but could not hear
Where scholars tapped to find his new remains
Gog and Magog ate pork
In vertical New York
And war began next Wednesday on the Danes.

The Glutton

The jowls of his belly crawl and swell like the sea
When his mandibles oily with lust champ and go wide;
Eternal, the springs of his spittle leak at the lips
Suspending the tongue like a whale that rolls on the tide,

His hands are as rotten fruit. His teeth are as corn.
Deep are the wells of his eyes and like navels, blind,
Dough is the brain that supplies his passion with bread,
Dough is the loose-slung sack of his great behind,

Will his paps become woman's? He dreams of the yielding of milk,
Despising the waste of his stool that recalls him to bread;
More than passion of sex and the transverse pains of disease
He thinks of starvation, the locked-up mouth of the dead.

I am glad that his stomach will eat him away in revenge,
Digesting itself when his blubber is lain in the earth.
Let the juice of his gluttony swallow him inward like lime
And leave of his volume only the mould of his girth.

Poet

Il arrive que l'esprit demande la poesie

Left leg flung out, head cocked to the right,
Tweed coat or army uniform, with book,
Beautiful eyes, who is this walking down?
Who, glancing at the pane of glass looks sharp
And thinks it is not he — as when a poet
Comes swiftly on some half-forgotten poem
And loosely holds the page, steady of mind,
      Thinking it is not his?

And when will *you* exist? — Oh, it is I,
Incredibly skinny, stooped, and neat as pie,
Ignorant as dirt, erotic as an ape,
Dreamy as puberty — with dirty hair!
Into the room like kangaroo he bounds,
Ears flopping like the most expensive hound's;
His chin receives all questions as he bows
      Mouthing a green bon-bon.

Has no more memory than rubber. Stands
Waist-deep in heavy mud of thought and broods
At his own wetness. When he would get out,
To his surprise he lifts in air a phrase
As whole and clean and silvery as a fish
Which jumps and dangles on his damned hooked grin,
But like a name-card on a man's lapel
      Calls him a conscious fool.

And child-like he remembers all his life
And cannily constructs it, fact by fact,
As boys paste postage stamps in careful books,
Denoting pence and legends and profiles,
Nothing more valuable. — And like a thief.
His eyes glassed over and congealed with guilt,
Fondles his secrets like a case of tools,
      And waits in empty doors.

By men despised for knowing what he is,
And by himself. But he exists for women.
As dolls to girls, as perfect wives to men,
So he to women. And to himself a thing,
All ages, epicene, without a trade.
To girls and wives always alive and fated;
To men and scholars always dead like Greek
        And always mistranslated.

Towards exile and towards shame he lures himself,
Tongue winding on his arm, and thinks like Eve
By biting apple will become most wise.
Sentio ergo sum: he feels his way
And words themselves stand up for him like Braille
And punch and perforate his parchment ear.
All language falls like Chinese on his soul,
        Image of song unsounded.

This is the coward's coward that in his dreams
Sees shapes of pain grow tall. Awake at night
He peers at sounds and stumbles at a breeze.
And none holds life less dear. For as a youth
Who by some accident observes his love
Naked and in some natural ugly act,
He turns with loathing and with flaming hands,
        Seared and betrayed by sight.

He is the business man, on beauty trades,
Dealer in arts and thoughts who, like the Jew,
Shall rise from slums and hated dialects
A tower of bitterness. Shall be always strange,
Hunted and then sought after. Shall be sat
Like an ambassador from another race
At tables rich with music. He shall eat flowers,
Chew honey and spit out gall. They shall all smile
        And love and pity him.

His death shall be by drowning. In that hour
When the last bubble of pure heaven's air
Hovers within his throat, safe on his bed,
A small eternal figurehead in terror,
He shall cry out and clutch his days of straw
Before the blackest wave. Lastly, his tomb
Shall list and founder in the troughs of grass
       And none shall speak his name.

Travelogue for Exiles

Look and remember. Look upon this sky;
Look deep and deep into the sea-clean air,
The unconfined, the terminus of prayer.
Speak now and speak into the hallowed dome.
What do you hear? What does the sky reply?
The heavens are taken: this is not your home.

Look and remember. Look upon this sea;
Look down and down into the tireless tide.
What of a life below, a life inside,
A tomb, a cradle in the curly foam?
The waves arise; sea-wind and sea agree
The waters are taken: this is not your home.

Look and remember. Look upon this land,
Far, far across the factories and the grass.
Surely, there, surely, they will let you pass.
Speak then and ask the forest and the loam.
What do you hear? What does the land command?
The earth is taken: this is not your home.

Midnight Show

The year is done, the last act of the vaudeville,
The last top hat and patent leather tappity-tap
Enclosed in darkness. Pat. Blackout. Only the organ
Groans, groans, its thousand golden throats in love;
While blue lowlight suffuses mysteries of sleep
Through racks of heads, and smoothly parts the gauzy veil
That slips, the last pretense of peace, into the wings.

With a raucous crash the music rises to its feet,
And pouring from the hidden eye like God the Light
The light white-molten cold fills out the vacant field
With shattered cities, striped ships, and maps with lines
That crawl — symbols of horror, symbols of obscenity;
A girl astride a giant cannon, holding a flag;
Removal of stone and stained-glass saints from a known cathedral;

And the Voice, the loving and faithful pointer, trots beside
Reel after reel, taking death in its well-trained stride.
The Voice, the polite, the auctioneer, places his hints
Like easy bids. The lab assistant, the Voice, dips
Their pity like litmus papers into His rancid heart. —
Dream to be surfeited, nerves clogged up with messages,
And, backed up at the ganglion, the news refused.

Dream to be out in snow where every corner Santa,
Heart of one generation's dreams, tinkles a bell.
We know him too. He is the Unemployed, but clowns
As the Giver, receiving pennies in a cast-iron pot.
Dream to be cold with Byrd at the world's bottom. Dream
To be warm in the Vatican, photographing a manuscript.
Dream to be there, a cell in Europe's poisoned blood.

Revulsion cannot rouse our heads for pride or protest.
The eye sees as the camera, a clean moronic gaze,
And to go is not impossible but merely careless.
O wife, what shall we tell the children that we saw?
O son, what shall we tell our father? And O my friend,
What shall we tell our senses when the lights go up
And noiselessly the golden curtains crash together!

Conscription Camp

Your landscape sickens with a dry disease
Even in May, Virginia, and your sweet pines
Like Frenchmen runted in a hundred wars
Are of a child's height in these battlefields.

For Wilson sowed his teeth where generals prayed
— High-sounding Lafayette and sick-eyed Lee —
The loud Elizabethan crashed your swamps
Like elephants and the subtle Indian fell,

Is it for love, you ancient-minded towns,
That on the tidy grass of your great graves
And on your roads and riverways serene
Between the corn with green flags in a row,

Wheat amorous as hair and hills like breasts
Each generation, ignorant of the last,
Mumbling in sheds, embarrassed to salute,
Comes back to choke on etiquette of hate?

You manufacture history like jute —
Labor is cheap, Virginia, for high deeds,
But in your British dream of reputation
The black man is your conscience and your cost.

Here on the plains perfect for civil war
The clapboard city like a weak mirage
Of order rises from the sand to house
These thousands and the paranoid Monroe;

The sunrise gun rasps in the throat of heaven;
The lungs of dawn are heavy and corrupt;
We hawk and spit; our flag walks through the air
Breathing hysteria thickly in each face.

Through the long school of day, absent in heart,
Distant in every thought but self we tread,
Wheeling in blocks like large expensive toys
That never understand except through fun.

To steal aside as aimlessly as curs
Is our desire; to stare at corporals
As sceptically as boys; not to believe
The misty-eyed letter and the cheap snapshot.

To cross the unnatural frontier of your name
Is our free dream, Virginia, and beyond,
White and unpatriotic in our beds,
To rise from sleep like driftwood out of surf.

But stricter than parole is this same wall
And these green clothes, a secret on the fields,
In towns betray us to the arresting touch
Of lady-wardens, good and evil wives.

And far and fabulous is the word "Outside"
Like "Europe" when the midnight liners sailed,
Leaving a wake of ermine on the tide
Where rubies drowned and eyes were softly drunk.

Still we abhor your news and every voice
Except the Personal Enemy's, and songs
That pumped by the great central heart of love
On tides of energy at evening come.

Instinctively to break your compact law
Box within box, Virginia, and throw down
The dangerous bright habits of pure form
We struggle hideously and cry for fear.

And like a very tired whore who stands
Wrapped in the sensual crimson of her art
High in the tired doorway of a street
And beckons half-concealed the passerby,

The sun, Virginia, on your Western stairs
Pauses and smiles away between the trees,
Motioning the soldier overhill to town
To his determined hungry burst of joy.

The Twins

Likeness has made them animal and shy.
See how they turn their full gaze left and right,
Seeking the other, yet not moving close;
Nothing in their relationship is gross,
But soft, conspicuous, like giraffes. And why
Do they not speak except by sudden sight?

Sisters kiss freely and unsubtle friends
Wrestle like lovers; brothers loudly laugh:
These in a dreamier bondage dare not touch.
Each is the other's soul and hears too much
The heartbeat of the other; each apprehends
The sad duality and the imperfect half.

The one lay sick, the other wandered free,
But like a child to a small plot confined
Walked a short way and dumbly reappeared.
Is it not all-in-all of what they feared,
The single death, the obvious destiny
That maims the miracle their will designed?

For they go emptily from face to face,
Keeping the instinctive partnership of birth
A ponderous marriage and a sacred name;
Theirs is the pride of shouldering each the same
The old indignity of Esau's race
And Dromio's denouement of tragic mirth.

Nostalgia

My soul stands at the window of my room,
   And I ten thousand miles away;
My days are filled with Ocean's sound of doom,
   Salt and cloud and the bitter spray.
Let the wind blow, for many a man shall die.

My selfish youth, my books with gilded edge,
   Knowledge and all gaze down the street;
The potted plants upon the window ledge
   Gaze down with selfish lives and sweet.
Let the wind blow, for many a man shall die.

My night is now her day, my day her night,
   So I lie down, and so I rise;
The sun burns close, the star is losing height,
   The clock is hunted down the skies.
Let the wind blow, for many a man shall die.

Truly a pin can make the memory bleed,
   A word explode the inward mind
And turn the skulls and flowers never freed
   Into the air, no longer blind.
Let the wind blow, for many a man shall die.

Laughter and grief join hands. Always the heart
   Clumps in the breast with heavy stride;
The face grows lined and wrinkled like a chart,
   The eyes bloodshot with tears and tide.
Let the wind blow, for many a man shall die.

A Cut Flower

I stand on slenderness all fresh and fair,
I feel root-firmness in the earth far down,
I catch in the wind and loose my scent for bees
That sack my throat for kisses and suck love.
What is the wind that brings thy body over?
Wind, I am beautiful and sick. I long
For rain that strikes and bites like cold and hurts.
Be angry, rain, for dew is kind to me
When I am cool from sleep and take my bath.

Who softens the sweet earth about my feet,
Touches my face so often and brings water?
Where does she go, taller than any sunflower
Over the grass like birds? Has she a root?
These are great animals that kneel to us,
Sent by the sun perhaps to help us grow.
I have seen death. The colors went away,
The petals grasped at nothing and curled tight.
Then the whole head fell off and left the sky.

She tended me and held me by my stalk.
Yesterday I was well, and then the gleam,
The thing sharper than frost cut me in half.
I fainted and was lifted high. I feel
Waist-deep in rain. My face is dry and drawn.
My beauty leaks into the glass like rain.
When first I opened to the sun I thought
My colors would be parched. Where are my bees?
Must I die now? Is this a part of life?

From
V-Letter and
Other Poems

(1944)

Troop Train

It stops the town we come through. Workers raise
Their oily arms in good salute and grin.
Kids scream as at a circus. Business men
Glance hopefully and go their measured way.
And women standing at their dumbstruck door
More slowly wave and seem to warn us back,
As if a tear blinding the course of war
Might once dissolve our iron in their sweet wish.

Fruit of the world, O clustered on ourselves
We hang as from a cornucopia
In total friendliness, with faces bunched
To spray the streets with catcalls and with leers.
A bottle smashes on the moving ties
And eyes fixed on a lady smiling pink
Stretch like a rubber-band and snap and sting
The mouth that wants the drink-of-water kiss.

And on through crummy continents and days,
Deliberate, grimy, slightly drunk we crawl,
The good-bad boys of circumstance and chance,
Whose bucket-helmets bang the empty wall
Where twist the murdered bodies of our packs
Next to the guns that only seem themselves.
And distance like a strap adjusted shrinks,
Tighten across the shoulder and holds firm.

Here is a deck of cards; out of this hand
Dealer, deal me my luck, a pair of bulls,
The right draw to a flush, the one-eyed jack.
Diamonds and hearts are red but spades are black,
And spades are spades and clubs are clovers — black.
But deal me winners, souvenirs of peace.
This stands to reason and arithmetic,
Luck also travels and not all come back.

Trains lead to ships and ships to death or trains,
And trains to death or trucks, and trucks to death,
Or trucks lead to the march, the march to death,
Or that survival which is all our hope;
And death leads back to trucks and trains and ships,
But life leads to the march, O flag! at last
The place of life found after trains and death —
Nightfall of nations brilliant after war.

Christmas Eve: Australia

The wind blows hot. English and foreign birds
And insects different as their fish excite
The would-be calm. The usual flocks and herds
Parade in permanent quiet out of sight,
And there one crystal like a grain of light
Sticks in the crucible of day and cools.
A cloud burnt to a crisp at some great height
Sips at the dark condensing in deep pools.

I smoke and read my Bible and chew gum,
Thinking of Christ and Christmas of last year,
And what those quizzical soldiers standing near
Ask of the war and Christmases to come,
And sick of causes and the tremendous blame
Curse lightly and pronounce your serious name.

Piano

The perfect ice of the thin keys must break
And fingers crash through stillness into sound,
And through the mahogany darkness of the lake
Splinter the muteness where all notes are found.
O white face floating upwards amidst hair!
Sweet hands entangled in the golden snare,
            Escape, escape, escape,
      Or in the coils of joy be drowned.

What is the cabinet that holds such speech
And is obedient to caresses strange
As tides that stroke the long-deserted beach,
And gales that scourge the Peruvian mountain range?
O flesh of wood with flanks aglow with suns,
O quivering as at the burst of monstrous guns,
            Subside, subside, subside,
      Or into dust and atoms change.

Nor can the note-shaped heart, nor can the ear
Withstand your praise, O numbers more appalling
Than ringed and voyaging on the atmosphere
Those heavy flocks of fallen angels falling;
You strike with fists of heaven against the void
Where all but choiring music is destroyed,
            And light, and light, and light,
      Bursts into voice forever calling.

Magician

Tall in his top hat, tall and alone in the room
Of aerial music, electric light
And the click of tables, the mephistophelian man
Toys with a wand and the wonders happen — for whom
And to what end the gleam of the shellacked
Trick within trick, as plain as black and white,
And all too clever, all too matter-of-fact
Like the sudden neatness of a shutting fan?

And somewhat sinister, like a millionaire
Or a poet or a street-corner quack
With a dollar bottle of cure . . . We are drawn to his eye
Only to stop at the eye we dare not dare;
We suspect and believe; *he* looks us out of face
And seems to say that magic is the knack
Of showing the result without a trace
Of the cause, end without means, what without why.

If now the amusing audience could see
His mangey unicorn that crops
The shabby velvet of his weariness,
An inch from the abyss of villainy,
The applause would freeze, the dust settle like snow,
And long before the asbestos curtain drops
Even the children would get up to go,
Be sick in the lobby, sob with young distress;

But fortunately they cannot. We proceed
Beyond the fire-eating, doves,
Padlocks, confetti, disappearing ropes,
To personal murder, the necessary deed
Of sawing a woman in half. We want her heart.
The sable executioner in gloves
Labors, but hoc est corpus! quite apart
She stands; we applaud our disappointed hopes.

And backstage somewhere, peeling his moustache,
He muses that he is an honest man
And wonders dramatically why. Deep in his ear
At times there sounds the subterranean plash
Of Alf and Phlegeton where tides revolve
With eyes of evil. There he first began;
There is the task he can no longer solve
But only wait for till his dying year.

Red Indian

To Jim Powell

Purest of breed of all the tribes
That trekked from time and took the Trail of Tears
There to the plain beyond the bribes
Of best advantage, past the rifle's reach,
Where instinct rests and action disappears
And the skulls of cattle bleach.

High in the plateaus of their soul
The silence is reshaped like rocks by wind,
Their eyes are beads that pay their toll,
Record the race-long heritage of grief,
At altitudes where memory is thinned,
Frown like a wrinkled chief.

The painted feather still upright
They walk in concrete Tulsa dark and mute,
Their bravest blankets slashing bright
The afternoon of progress and of wives;
Their children glow like some primordial fruit
Cut from the branch by knives.

Bark-smooth as spears and arrow-straight
They watch the world like winter trees and grow;
Forests of them revive and wait,
In timeless hibernation dream and stir.
These are the lives that love the soundless snow
And wear the wind like fur.

Because their pride of nation leaps,
The august rivers where they yelled and died
Move with a blood that never sleeps.
Because their nature suffers the arrest
Of seed, their silence crowds us like a tide
And moves their mournful quest.

Full Moon: New Guinea

These nights we fear the aspects of the moon,
Sleep lightly in the radiance falling clear
On palms and ferns and hills and us; for soon
The small burr of the bombers in our ear
Tickles our rest; we rise as from a nap
And take our helmets absently and meet,
Prepared for any spectacle or mishap,
At trenches fresh and narrow at our feet.

Look up, look up, and wait and breathe. These nights
We fear Orion and the Cross. The crowd
Of deadly insects caught in our long lights
Glitter and seek to burrow in a cloud
Soft-minded with high explosive. Breathe and wait,
The bombs are falling darkly for our fate.

The Gun

You were angry and manly to shatter the sleep of your throat;
The kiss of your blast is upon me, O friend of my fear,
And I savour your breath like a perfume as salt and austere
As the scent of the thunder of heaven that brims in the moat!

I grip you. We lie on the ground in the thongs of our clasp
And we stare like the hunter who starts at a tenuous cry;
We have wounded the wind with a wire and stung in the sky
A white hole that is small and unseen as the bite of the asp.

The smooth of your cheek — Do you sight from the depth of your eye
More faultless than vision, more true than the aiming of stars?
Is the heart of your hatred the target of redness of Mars
Or the roundness of heart of the one who must stumble and die?

O the valley is silent and shocked. I absolve from your name
The exaction of murder, my gun. It is I who have killed.
It is I whose enjoyment of horror is fine and fulfilled.
You are only the toy of my terror, my emblem of blame.

Come with me. We shall creep for his eyes like the sweat of my skin,
For the wind is repaired and the fallen is calling for breath.
You are only the means of the practical humor of death
Which is savage to punish the dead for the sake of my sin!

The Second-Best Bed

In the name of the almighty God, amen,
  I, William Shakespeare, take my pen
  And do bequeath in perfect health
To Christ my soul and to my kin my wealth
      When I am dead.
      And to Anne, good dame,
      I bequeath my name,
A table, a chair, and the second-best bed.

To Judith a hundred fifty pounds I give,
  The same if three more years she live,
  And the broad-edge silver bowl. To Joan
My hose and clothes and all the suits I own
      Both blue and red.
      And to Anne, good dame,
      I bequeath my name,
A table, a chair, and the second-best bed.

Ten pounds to beggars for their drink and board,
  To Mr. Thomas Cole my sword,
  To Richard Burbage, Cundell, Nash,
Heminge and Hamlet one pound six in cash,
      And to her I wed
      Who is Anne, good dame,
      I bequeath my name,
A table, a chair, and the second-best bed.

To Joan also my Stratford house I will,
  For sisters shall not go with nil,
  And to her sons five pounds apiece
To be paid within a year of my decease.
      And as I have said
      To Anne, good dame,
      I bequeath my name,
A table, a chair, and the second-best bed.

Last, to my daughter, born Susanna Hall,
   My barns and stables, lands and all,
   Tenements, orchards, jewels, and wares,
All these forever for herself and heirs,
         Till all are dead;
         But to Anne, good dame,
         I bequeath my name,
A table, a chair, and the second-best bed.

Good wife, bad fortune is to blame
That I bequeath, when I am dead,
To you my honor and my name,
A table, a chair, and the second-best bed.

Fireworks

In midsummer darkness when primeval silences close
On the women in linen and children and husbands in blouses
We gather in laughter and move with a current that flows
Through the intimate suburbs of ice-cream and talkative houses

To a fabulous field of the night of the rainbows of ages
Where blindness is dyed with the blooms and the tints of desire,
And the wars of our boyhood rise up from the oldest of pages
With heroes erected on billboards of fuses and wire.

In the garden of pleistocene flowers we wander like Alice
Where seed sends a stalk in the heavens and pops from a pod
A blue blossom that hangs on the distance and opens its chalice
And falls in the dust of itself and goes out with a nod.

How the hairy tarantulas crawl in the soft of the ether
Where showers of lilies explode in the jungle of creepers;
How the rockets of sperm hurtle up to the moon and beneath her
Deploy for the eggs of the astral and sorrowful sleepers!

And the noble bombardment that bursts in the depth of our ears
Lifts the hair of our heads and interprets in absolute noises
The brimstone of total destruction, the doom of our years.
O the Judgment that shatters the rose of our secrets and poises!

In Niagaras of fire we leak in the luminous aura
And gasp at the portrait of Lincoln alive on the lattice.
Our history hisses and spits in the burning Gomorrah,
The volcanoes subside; we are given our liberty gratis.

Lord, I Have Seen Too Much

Lord, I have seen too much for one who sat
In quiet at his window's luminous eye
And puzzled over house and street and sky,
Safe only in the narrowest habitat;
Who studied peace as if the world were flat,
The edge of nature linear and dry,
But faltered at each brilliant entity
Drawn like a prize from some magician's hat.

Too suddenly this lightning is disclosed:
Lord, in a day the vacuum of Hell,
The mouth of blood, the ocean's ragged jaw,
More than embittered Adam ever saw
When driven from Eden to the East to dwell,
The lust of godhead hideously exposed!

Franklin

The star of Reason, Ben, reposed in you
Octagon spectacles, a sparking kite,
Triggers and jiggers, bobbins, reels and screws,
And aphorisms spelled in black and white.

Wiseacre, editor, and diplomat,
First of the salesmen, hero of the clerk,
The logic of invention led to bells
Joyous for George and terrible for Burke.

Poor Richard prospers and the grocery man
Has your disarming prose and pays his tax.
Sir, what is the reason for this bird
That sings and screams and coos and crows and quacks?

Two-penny buns, a whistle for the boy,
Rare Ben, the printer's devil used you well.
Lenin and Freud embroider left and right
And Curtis beats The Independence Bell.

Jefferson

If vision can dilate, my noble lord,
Farther than porticos, Italian cells,
Newtonian gardens, Haydn, and cuisine,
Tell us, most serious of all our poets,
Why is the clock so low?

I see the tender gradient of your will;
Virginia is the Florence of your soul,
Yes, ours. The architecture of your hands
Quiets ambition and revives our skill
And buys our faithlessness.

So temperate, so remote, so sure of phrase,
Your music sweeps a continent, a sphere,
Fashions a modern language for a war
And by its cadence makes responsible
Our million names to you.

When you were old the god of government
Seemed to recede a pace, and you were glad.
You watched the masons through your telescope
Finish your school of freedom. Death itself
Stood thoughtful at your bed.

And now the surfaces of mind are rubbed
Our essence starts like serum from our eyes.
How can you not assume the deities
That move behind the bloodshot look and lean
Like saints and Salem devils?

Sunday: New Guinea

The bugle sounds the measured call to prayers,
The band starts bravely with a clarion hymn,
From every side, singly, in groups, in pairs,
Each to his kind of service comes to worship Him.

Our faces washed, our hearts in the right place,
We kneel or stand or listen from our tents;
Half-naked natives with their kind of grace
Move down the road with balanced staffs like mendicants.

And over the hill the guns bang like a door
And planes repeat their mission in the heights.
The jungle outmaneuvers creeping war
And crawls within the circle of our sacred rites.

I long for our disheveled Sundays home,
Breakfast, the comics, news of latest crimes,
Talk without reference, and palindromes,
Sleep and the Philharmonic and the ponderous *Times*.

I long for lounging in the afternoons
Of clean intelligent warmth, my brother's mind,
Books and thin plates and flowers and shining spoons,
And your love's presence, snowy, beautiful, and kind.

Jew

The name is immortal but only the name, for the rest
Is a nose that can change in the weathers of time or persist
Or die out in confusion or model itself on the best.

But the name is a language itself that is whispered and hissed
Through the houses of ages, and ever a language the same,
And ever and ever a blow on our heart like a fist.

And this last of our dream in the desert, O curse of our name,
Is immortal as Abraham's voice in our fragment of prayer
Adonai, Adonai, for our bondage of murder and shame!

And the word for the murder of God will cry out on the air
Though the race is no more and the temples are closed of our will
And the peace is made fast on the earth and the earth is made fair;

Our name is impaled in the heart of the world on a hill
Whether we suffer to die by the hands of ourselves, and to kill.

Shylock

Ho, no, no, no, no, my meaning in saying he is a good
man is to have you understand me, that he is sufficient.
— *The Merchant of Venice*

Home from the court he locked the door and sat
In the evil darkness, suddenly composed.
The knife shone dimly on the table and his eyes
Like candles in an empty room
Shone hard at nothing. Yet he appeared to smile.

Then he took up his talith and his hat
And prayed mechanically and absently closed
His fingers on the knife. If he could realize
His actual defeat or personal doom
He must die or change or show that he was vile.

Nevertheless he would remain and live,
Submit to baptism, pay his fines,
Appear in the Rialto as early as tomorrow,
Not innocently but well aware
That his revenge is an accomplished fact.

And poverty itself would help to give
Humility to his old designs.
His fallen reputation would help borrow
A credit of new hate; for nothing will repair
This open breach of nature, cruel and wracked.

His daughter lies with swine, and the old rat
Tubal will be obsequious
To buy off his disgrace and bargain on his shame.
Despair can teach him nothing at all:
Gold he hates more than he hates Jesus' crown.

The logic of Balthasar will fall flat
On heaven's hearing. Incurious
As to the future, totally clear of blame,
He takes his ledgers out of the wall
And lights them with a taper and sits down.

The Synagogue

The synagogue dispirits the deep street,
Shadows the face of the pedestrian,
It is the adumbration of the Wall,
The stone survival that laments itself,
Our old entelechy of stubborn God,
Our calendar that marks a separate race.

The swift cathedral palpitates the blood,
The soul moves upward like a wing to meet
The pinnacles of saints. There flocks of thanks
In nooks of holy tracery arrive
And rested take their message in mid-air
Sphere after sphere into the papal heaven.

The altar of the Hebrews is a house,
No relic but a place, Sinai itself,
Not holy ground but factual holiness
Wherein the living god is resident.
Our scrolls are volumes of the thundered law
Sabbath by sabbath wound by hand to read.

He knows Al-Eloah to whom the Arab
Barefooted falls on sands, on table roofs,
In latticed alleys underneath the egg
On wide mosaics, when the crier shrills.
O profitable curse, most sacred rug,
Your book is blindness and your sword is rust.

And Judenhetze is the course of time;
We were rebellious, all but Abraham,
And skulked like Jonah, angry at the gourd.
Our days are captives in the minds of kings,
We stand in tens disjointed on the world
Grieving the ribbon of a coast we hated.

Some choose the ethics of belief beyond
Even particular election. Some
In bland memorial churches modify
The architecture of the state, and heaven
Disfranchised watches, caput mortuum,
The human substance eating, voting, smiling.

The Jew has no bedecked magnificat
But sits in stricken ashes after death,
Refusing grace; his grace is flowerless,
He gutters in the tallow of his name.
At Rome the multiplying tapers sing
Life endless in the history of art.

And Zion womanless refuses grace
To the first woman as to Magdalene,
But half-remembers Judith or Rahab,
The shrewd good heart of Esther honors still,
And weeps for almost sacred Ruth, but doubts
Either full harlotry or the faultless birth.

Our wine is wine, our bread is harvest bread
That feeds the body and is not the body.
Our blessing is to wine but not the blood
Nor to sangreal the sacred dish. We bless
The whiteness of the dish and bless the water
And are not anthropophagous to him.

The immanent son then came as one of us
And stood against the ark. We have no prophets,
Our scholars are afraid. There have been friars,
Great healers, poets. The stars were terrible.
At the Sadducee court he touched our panic;
We were betrayed to sacrifice this man.

We live by virtue of philosophy,
Past love, and have our devious reward.
For faith he gave us land and took the land,
Thinking us exiles of all humankind.
Our name is yet the identity of God
That storms the falling altar of the world.

The Interlude

I

Much of transfiguration that we hear,
The ballet of the atoms, the second law
Of thermo-dynamics, Isis, and the queer

Fertilization of fish, the Catholic's awe
For the life-cycle of the Nazarene,
His wife whom sleeping Milton thought he saw;

Much of the resurrection that we've seen
And taken part in, like the Passion Play,
All of autumnal red and April green,

To those who walk in work from day to day,
To economic and responsible man,
All, all is substance. Life that lets him stay

Uses his substance kindly while she can
But drops him lifeless after his one span.

II

What lives? the proper creatures in their homes?
A weed? the white and giddy butterfly?
Bacteria? necklaces of chromosomes?

What lives? the breathing bell of the clear sky?
The crazed bull of the sea? Andean crags?
Armies that plunge into themselves to die?

People? A sacred relic wrapped in rags,
The ham-bone of a saint, the winter rose,
Do these? — And is there not a hand that drags

The bottom of the universe for those
Who still perhaps are breathing? Listen well,
There lives a quiet like a cathedral close

At the soul's center where substance cannot dwell
And life flowers like music from a bell.

III

Writing, I crushed an insect with my nail
And thought nothing at all. A bit of wing
Caught my eye then, a gossamer so frail

And exquisite, I saw in it a thing
That scorned the grossness of the thing I wrote.
It hung upon my finger like a sting.

A leg I noticed next, fine as a mote,
"And on this frail eyelash he walked," I said,
"And climbed and walked like any mountain-goat."

And in this mood I sought the little head,
But it was lost; then in my heart a fear
Cried out, "A life — why beautiful, why dead!"

It was a mite that held itself most dear,
So small I could have drowned it with a tear.

The Intellectual

What should the wars do with these jigging fools?

The man behind the book may not be man,
His own man or the book's or yet the time's,
But still be whole, deciding what he can
In praise of politics or German rimes;

But the intellectual lights a cigarette
And offers it lit to the lady, whose odd smile
Is the merest hyphen — lest he should forget
What he has been resuming all the while.

He talks to overhear, she to withdraw
To some interior feminine fireside
Where the back arches, beauty puts forth a paw
Like a black puma stretching in velvet pride,

Making him think of cats, a stray of which
Some days sets up a howling in his brain,
Pure interference such as this neat bitch
Seems to create from listening disdain.

But talk is all the value, the release,
Talk is the very fillip of an act,
The frame and subject of the masterpiece
Under whose film of age the face is cracked.

His own forehead glows like expensive wood,
But back of it the mind is disengaged,
Self-sealing clock recording bad and good
At constant temperature, intact, unaged.

But strange, his body is an open house
Inviting every passerby to stay;
The city to and fro beneath his brows
Wanders and drinks and chats from night to day.

Think of a private thought, indecent room
Where one might kiss his daughter before bed!
Life is embarrassed; shut the family tomb.
Console your neighbor for his recent dead;

Do something! die in Spain or paint a green
Gouache, go into business (Rimbaud did),
Or start another Little Magazine,
Or move in with a woman, have a kid.

Invulnerable, impossible, immune,
Do what you will, your will will not be done
But dissipate the light of afternoon
Till evening flickers like the midnight sun,

And midnight shouts and dies: I'd rather be
A milkman walking in his sleep at dawn
Bearing fat quarts of cream, and so be free,
Crossing alone and cold from lawn to lawn.

I'd rather be a barber and cut hair
Than walk with you in gilt museum halls,
You and the puma-lady, she so rare
Exhaling her silk soul upon the walls.

Go take yourselves apart, but let me be
The fault you find with everyman. I spit,
I laugh, I fight; and you, *l'homme qui rît*,
Swallow your stale saliva, and still sit.

V-Letter

I love you first because your face is fair,
      Because your eyes Jewish and blue,
Set sweetly with the touch of foreignness
Above the cheekbones, stare rather than dream.
Often your countenance recalls a boy
      Blue-eyed and small, whose silent mischief
Tortured his parents and compelled my hate
        To wish his ugly death.
Because of this reminder, my soul's trouble,
And for your face, so often beautiful,
        I love you, wish you life.

I love you first because you wait, because
      For your own sake, I cannot write
Beyond these words. I love you for these words
That sting and creep like insects and leave filth.
I love you for the poverty you cry
      And I bend down with tears of steel
That melt your hand like wax, not for this war
        The droplets shattering
Those candle-glowing fingers of my joy,
But for your name of agony, my love,
        That cakes my mouth with salt.

And all your imperfections and perfections
      And all your magnitude of grace
And all this love explained and unexplained
Is just a breath. I see you woman-size
And this looms larger and more goddess-like
      Than silver goddesses on screens.
I see you in the ugliness of light,
       Yet you are beautiful,
And in the dark of absence your full length
Is such as meets my body to the full
        Though I am starved and huge.

You turn me from these days as from a scene
        Out of an open window far
Where lies the foreign city and the war.
You are my home and in your spacious love
I dream to march as under flaring flags
        Until the door is gently shut.
Give me the tearless lesson of your pride,
                Teach me to live and die
As one deserving anonymity,
The mere devotion of a house to keep
        A woman and a man.

Give me the free and poor inheritance
        Of our own kind, not furniture
Of education, nor the prophet's pose,
The general cause of words, the hero's stance,
The ambitions incommensurable with flesh,
        But the drab makings of a room
Where sometimes in the afternoon of thought
        The brief and blinding flash
May light the enormous chambers of your will
And show the gracious Parthenon that time
        Is ever measured by.

As groceries in a pantry gleam and smile
        Because they are important weights
Bought with the metal minutes of your pay,
So do these hours stand in solid rows,
The dowry for a use in common life.
        I love you first because your years
Lead to my matter-of-fact and simple death
        Or to our open marriage,
And I pray nothing for my safety back,
Not even luck, because our love is whole
        Whether I live or fail.

Elegy for a Dead Soldier

I

A white sheet on the tail-gate of a truck
Becomes an altar; two small candlesticks
Sputter at each side of the crucifix
Laid round with flowers brighter than the blood,
Red as the red of our apocalypse,
Hibiscus that a marching man will pluck
To stick into his rifle or his hat,
And great blue morning-glories pale as lips
That shall no longer taste or kiss or swear.
The wind begins a low magnificat,
The chaplain chats, the palmtrees swirl their hair,
The columns come together through the mud.

II

We too are ashes as we watch and hear
The psalm, the sorrow, and the simple praise
Of one whose promised thoughts of other days
Were such as ours, but now wholly destroyed,
The service record of his youth wiped out,
His dream dispersed by shot, must disappear.
What can we feel but wonder at a loss
That seems to point at nothing but the doubt
Which flirts our sense of luck into the ditch?
Reader of Paul who prays beside this fosse,
Shall we believe our eyes or legends rich
With glory and rebirth beyond the void?

III

For this comrade is dead, dead in the war,
A young man out of millions yet to live,
One cut away from all that war can give,
Freedom of self and peace to wander free.
Who mourns in all this sober multitude
Who did not feel the bite of it before
The bullet found its aim? This worthy flesh,
This boy laid in a coffin and reviewed —
Who has not wrapped himself in this same flag,
Heard the light fall of dirt, his wound still fresh,
Felt his eyes closed, and heard the distant brag
Of the last volley of humanity?

IV

By chance I saw him die, stretched on the ground,
A tattooed arm lifted to take the blood
Of someone else sealed in a tin. I stood
During the last delirium that stays
The intelligence a tiny moment more,
And then the strangulation, the last sound.
The end was sudden, like a foolish play,
A stupid fool slamming a foolish door,
The absurd catastrophe, half-prearranged,
And all the decisive things still left to say.
So we disbanded, angrier and unchanged,
Sick with the utter silence of dispraise.

V

We ask for no statistics of the killed,
For nothing political impinges on
This single casualty, or all those gone,
Missing or healing, sinking or dispersed,
Hundreds of thousands counted, millions lost.
More than an accident and less than willed
Is every fall, and this one like the rest.
However others calculate the cost,
To us the final aggregate is *one*,
One with a name, one transferred to the blest;
And though another stoops and takes the gun,
We cannot add the second to the first.

VI

I would not speak for him who could not speak
Unless my fear were true: he was not wronged,
He knew to which decision he belonged
But let it choose itself. Ripe in instinct,
Neither the victim nor the volunteer,
He followed, and the leaders could not seek
Beyond the followers. Much of this he knew;
The journey was a detour that would steer
Into the Lincoln Highway of a land
Remorselessly improved, excited, new,
And that was what he wanted. He had planned
To earn and drive. He and the world had winked.

VII

No history deceived him, for he knew
Little of times and armies not his own;
He never felt that peace was but a loan,
Had never questioned the idea of gain.
Beyond the headlines once or twice he saw
The gathering of a power by the few
But could not tell their names; he cast his vote,
Distrusting all the elected but not law.
He laughed at socialism; *on mourrait*
Pour les industriels? He shed his coat
And not for brotherhood, but for his pay.
To him the red flag marked the sewer main.

VIII

Above all else he loathed the homily,
The slogan and the ad. He paid his bill,
But not for Congressmen at Bunker Hill.
Ideals were few and those there were not made
For conversation. He belonged to church
But never spoke of God. The Christmas tree,
The Easter egg, baptism, he observed,
Never denied the preacher on his perch,
And would not sign Resolved That or Whereas.
Softness he had and hours and nights reserved
For thinking, dressing, dancing to the jazz.
His laugh was real, his manners were homemade.

IX

Of all men poverty pursued him least;
He was ashamed of all the down and out,
Spurned the panhandler like an uneasy doubt,
And saw the unemployed as a vague mass
Incapable of hunger or revolt.
He hated other races, south or east,
And shoved them to the margin of his mind.
He could recall the justice of the Colt,
Take interest in a gang-war like a game.
His ancestry was somewhere far behind
And left him only his peculiar name.
Doors opened, and he recognized no class.

X

His children would have known a heritage,
Just or unjust, the richest in the world,
The quantum of all art and science curled
In the horn of plenty, bursting from the horn,
A people bathed in honey, Paris come,
Vienna transferred with the highest wage,
A World's Fair spread to Phoenix, Jacksonville,
Earth's capital, the new Byzantium,
Kingdom of man — who knows? Hollow or firm,
No man can ever prophesy until
Out of our death some undiscovered germ,
Whole toleration or pure peace is born.

XI

The time to mourn is short that best becomes
The military dead. We lift and fold the flag,
Lay bare the coffin with its written tag,
And march away. Behind, four others wait
To lift the box, the heaviest of loads.
The anesthetic afternoon benumbs,
Sickens our senses, forces back our talk.
We know that others on tomorrow's roads
Will fall, ourselves perhaps, the man beside,
Over the world the threatened, all who walk:
And could we mark the grave of him who died
We would write this beneath his name and date:

EPITAPH

Underneath this wooden cross there lies
A Christian killed in battle. You who read,
Remember that this stranger died in pain;
And passing here, if you can lift your eyes
Upon a peace kept by a human creed,
Know that one soldier has not died in vain.

From
Trial of a Poet
(1947)

Homecoming

Lost in the vastness of the void Pacific
My thousand days of exile, pain,
Bid me farewell. Gone is the Southern Cross
To her own sky, fallen a continent
Under the wave, dissolved the bitterest isles
In their salt element,
And here upon the deck the mist encloses
My smile that would light up all darkness
And ask forgiveness of the things that thrust
Shame and all death on millions and on me.

We bring no raw materials from the East
But green-skinned men in blue-lit holds
And lunatics impounded between-decks;
The mighty ghoul-ship that we ride exhales
The sickly-sweet stench of humiliation,
And even the majority, untouched by steel
Or psychoneurosis, stare with eyes in rut,
Their hands a rabble to snatch the riches
Of glittering shops and girls.

Because I am angry at this kindness which
Is both habitual and contradictory
To the life of armies, now I stand alone
And hate the swarms of khaki men that crawl
Like lice upon the wrinkled hide of earth,
Infesting ships as well. Not otherwise
Could I lean outward piercing fog to find
Our sacred bridge of exile and return.
My tears are psychological, not poems
To the United States; my smile is prayer.

Gnawing the thin slops of anxiety,
Escorted by the groundswell and by gulls,
In silence and with mystery we enter
The territorial waters. Not till then
Does that convulsive terrible joy, more sudden
And brilliant than the explosion of a ship,
Shatter the tensions of the heaven and sea
To crush a hundred thousand skulls
And liberate in that high burst of love
The imprisoned souls of soldiers and of me.

The Conscientious Objector

The gates clanged and they walked you into jail
More tense than felons but relieved to find
The hostile world shut out, the flags that dripped
From every mother's windowpane, obscene
The bloodlust sweating from the public heart,
The dog authority slavering at your throat.
A sense of quiet, of pulling down the blind
Possessed you. Punishment you felt was clean.

The decks, the catwalks, and the narrow light
Composed a ship. This was a mutinous crew
Troubling the captains for plain decencies,
A Mayflower brim with pilgrims headed out
To establish new theocracies to west,
A Noah's ark coasting the topmost seas
Ten miles above the sodomites and fish.
These inmates loved the only living doves.

Like all men hunted from the world you made
A good community, voyaging the storm
To no safe Plymouth or green Ararat;
Trouble or calm, the men with Bibles prayed,
The gaunt politicals construed our hate.
The opposite of all armies, you were best
Opposing uniformity and yourselves;
Prison and personality were your fate.

You suffered not so physically but knew
Maltreatment, hunger, ennui of the mind.
Well might the soldier kissing the hot beach
Erupting in his face damn all your kind.
Yet you who saved neither yourselves nor us
Are equally with those who shed the blood
The heroes of our cause. Your conscience is
What we come back to in the armistice.

The Progress of Faust

He was born in Deutschland, as you would suspect,
And graduated in magic from Cracow
In Fifteen Five. His portraits show a brow
Heightened by science. The eye is indirect,
As of bent light upon a crooked soul,
And that he bargained with the Prince of Shame
For pleasures intellectually foul
Is known by every court that lists his name.

His frequent disappearances are put down
To visits in the regions of the damned
And to the periodic deaths he shammed,
But, unregenerate and in Doctor's gown,
He would turn up to lecture at the fair
And do a minor miracle for a fee.
Many a life he whispered up the stair
To teach the black art of anatomy.

He was as deaf to angels as an oak
When, in the fall of Fifteen Ninety-four,
He went to London and crashed through the floor
In mock damnation of the playgoing folk.
Weekending with the scientific crowd,
He met Sir Francis Bacon and helped draft
"Colours of Good and Evil" and read aloud
An obscene sermon at which no one laughed.

He toured the Continent for a hundred years
And subsidized among the peasantry
The puppet play, his tragic history;
With a white glove he boxed the devil's ears
And with a black his own. Tired of this,
He published penny poems about his sins,
In which he placed the heavy emphasis
On the white glove which, for a penny, wins.

Some time before the hemorrhage of the Kings
Of France, he turned respectable and taught;
Quite suddenly everything that he had thought
Seemed to grow scholars' beards and angels' wings.
It was the Overthrow. On Reason's throne
He sat with the fair Phrygian on his knees
And called all universities his own,
As plausible a figure as you please.

Then back to Germany as the sages' sage
To preach comparative science to the young
Who came from every land in a great throng
And knew they heard the master of the age.
When for a secret formula he paid
The Devil another fragment of his soul,
His scholars wept, and several even prayed
That Satan would restore him to them whole.

Backwardly tolerant, Faustus was expelled
From the Third Reich in Nineteen Thirty-nine.
His exit caused the breaching of the Rhine,
Except for which the frontier might have held.
Five years unknown to enemy and friend
He hid, appearing on the sixth to pose
In an American desert at war's end
Where, at his back, a dome of atoms rose.

In the Waxworks

At midday when the light rebukes the world,
Searching the seams of faces, cracks of walls
And each fault of the beautiful,
Seized by a panic of the street I fled
Into a waxworks where the elite in crime
And great in fame march past in fixed parade.
How pale they were beneath their paint, how pure
The monsters gleaming from the cubicles!

When, as in torsion, I beheld
These malformations of the evil mind
I grew serene and seemed to fall in love,
As one retiring to a moving picture
Or to a gallery of art. I saw
The basest plasm of the human soul
Here turned to sculpture, fingering,
Kissing, and corrupting life.

So back and forth among the leers of wax
I strutted for the idols of the tribe,
Aware that I was on display, not they,
And that I had come down to pray,
As one retires to a synagogue
Or to a plaster saint upon the wall.
Why were these effigies more dear to me
Than haughty mannikins in a window-shop?

I said a rosary for the Presidents
And fell upon my knees before
The Ripper and an exhibit of disease
Revolting more in its soft medium
Than in the flesh. I stroked a prince's hand,
Leaving a thumbprint in the palm. I swore
Allegiance to the suicide whose wrists
Of tallow bled with admirable red.

Why were these images more dear to me
Than faïence dolls or gods of smooth Pentelikon?
Because all statuary turns to death
And only half-art balances.
The fetish lives, idolatry is true,
The crude conception of the putrid face
Sticks to my heart. This criminal in wan
Weak cerement of translucent fat

Is my sweet saint. O heretic, O mute,
When broils efface the Metropolitan
And swinish man from some cloaca creeps
Or that deep midden, his security,
Coming to you in brutish admiration
May he look soft into your eyes;
And you, good wax, may you not then despise
Our sons and daughters, fallen apes.

D.C.

The bad breed of the natives with their hates
That border on a Georgian night,
The short vocabulary, the southern look
That writes a volume on your past, the men
Freeholders of the city-state, the women
Polite for murder — these happen to be;
The rest arrive and never quite remain.

The rest live with an easy homelessness
And common tastelessness, their souls
Weakly lit up by blazing screens and tales
Told by a newspaper. Holidays the vast
Basilicas of the railroad swallow up
Hundreds of thousands, struggling in the tide
For home, the one identity and past.

The noble riches keep themselves, the miles
Of marble breast the empty wind,
The halls of books and pictures manufacture
Their deep patinas, the fountains coldly splash
To the lone sailor, the boulevards stretch out
Farther than Arlington, where all night long
One living soldier marches for the dead.

Only the very foreign, the very proud,
The richest and the very poor
Hid in their creepy purlieus white or black
Adore this whole Augustan spectacle,
And chancelleries perceive the porch of might
Surmounted by the dome in which there lies
No Bonaparte, no Lenin, but a floor.

Yet those who govern live in quaintness, close
In the Georgian ghetto of the best;
What was the simplest of the old becomes
The exquisite palate of the new. Their names
Are admirals and paternalists, their ways
The ways of Lee who, having lost the slaves,
Died farther south, a general in the wrong.

The Convert

Deep in the shadowy bethel of the tired mind,
Where spooks and death lights ride, and Marys, too,
Materialize like senseless ectoplasm
Smiling in blue, out of the blue,
Quite gradually, on a common afternoon,
With no more inner fanfare than a sigh,
With no cross in the air, drizzle of blood,
Beauty of blinding voices from up high,
The man surrenders reason to the ghost
And enters church, via the vestry room.

The groan of positive science, hiss of friends,
Substantiate what doctors call
His rather shameful and benign disease,
But ecumenical heaven clearly sees
His love, his possibilities.
O victory of the Unintelligence,
What mystic rose developing from rock
Is more a miracle than this overthrow?
What Constitution ever promised more
Than his declared insanity?

Yet he shall be less perfect than before,
Being no longer neutral to the Book
But answerable. What formerly were poems,
Precepts, and commonplaces now are laws,
Dantean atlases, and official news.
The dust of ages settles on his mind
And in his ears he hears the click of beads
Adding, adding, adding like a prayer machine
His heartfelt sums. Upon his new-found knees
He treasures up the gold of never-ending day.

All arguments are vain — that Notre Dame
Has plumbing, Baptists shoot their fellowmen,
Hindus are pious, nuns have Cadillacs.
Apologetics anger him who is
The living proof of what he newly knows;
And proudly sorrowing for those who fail
To read his simple summa theologica,
He prays that in the burning they be spared,
And prays for mercy as the south wind blows,
And for all final sins that tip the scale.

Peace on a hundred thousand temples falls
With gently even light, revealing some
With wounded walls and missing faces, some
Spared by the bombardier, and some by God.
In mournful happiness the clerics move
To put the altars back, and the new man,
Heartbroken, walks among the broken saints,
Thinking how heavy is the hand that hates,
How light and secret is the sign of love
In the hour of many significant conversions.

Boy-Man

England's lads are miniature men
To start with, grammar in their shiny hats,
And serious: in America who knows when
Manhood begins? Presidents dance and hug
And while the kind King waves and gravely chats
American wets on England's old green rug.

The boy-man roars. Worry alone will give
This one the verisimilitude of age.
Those white teeth are his own, for he must live
Longer, grow taller than the Texas race.
Fresh are his eyes, his darkening skin the gauge
Of bloods that freely mix beneath his face.

He knows the application of the book
But not who wrote it; shuts it like a shot.
Rather than read he thinks that he will look,
Rather than look he thinks that he will talk,
Rather than talk he thinks that he will not
Bother at all; would rather ride than walk.

His means of conversation is the joke,
Humor his language underneath which lies
The undecoded dialect of the folk.
Abroad he scorns the foreigner: what's old
Is worn, what's different bad, what's odd unwise.
He gives off heat and is enraged by cold.

Charming, becoming to the suits he wears,
The boy-man, younger than his eldest son,
Inherits the state; upon his silver hairs
Time like a panama hat sits at a tilt
And smiles. To him the world has just begun
And every city waiting to be built.

Mister, remove your shoulder from the wheel
And say this prayer, "Increase my vitamins,
Make my decisions of the finest steel,
Pour motor oil upon my troubled spawn,
Forgive the Europeans for their sins,
Establish them, that values may go on."

The Southerner

He entered with the authority of politeness
And the jokes died in the air. A well-made blaze
Grew round the main log in the fireplace
Spontaneously. I watched its brightness
Spread to the altered faces of my guests.
They did not like the Southerner. I did.
A liberal felt that someone should forbid
That soft voice making its soft arrests.

As when a Negro or a prince extends
His hand to an average man, and the mind
Speeds up a minute and then drops behind,
So did the conversation of my friends.
I was amused by this respectful awe
Which those hotly deny who have no prince.
I watched the frown, the stare, and the wince
Recede into attention, the arms thaw.

I saw my southern evil memories
Raped from my mind before my eyes, my youth
Practicing caste, perfecting the untruth
Of staking honor on the wish to please.
I saw my honor's paradox:
Grandpa, the saintly Jew, keeping his beard
In difficult Virginia, yet endeared
Of blacks and farmers, although orthodox.

The nonsense of the gracious lawn,
The fall of hollow columns in the pines,   •
Do these deceive more than the rusted signs
Of Jesus on the road? Can they go on
In the timeless manner of all gentlefolk
There in a culture rotted and unweeded
Where the black yoni of the South is seeded
By crooked men in denims thin as silk?

They do go on, denying still the fall
Of Richmond and man, who gently live
On the street above the violence, fugitive,
Graceful, and darling, who recall
The heartbroken country once about to flower,
Full of black poison, beautiful to smell,
Who know how to conform, how to compel,
And how from the best bush to receive a flower.

Recapitulations

I

I was born downtown on a wintry day
    And under the roof where Poe expired;
Tended by nuns my mother lay
    Dark-haired and beautiful and tired.

Doctors and cousins paid their call,
    The rabbi and my father helped.
A crucifix burned on the wall
    Of the bright room where I was whelped.

At one week all my family prayed,
    Stuffed wine and cotton in my craw;
The rabbi blessed me with a blade
    According to the Mosaic Law.

The white steps blazed in Baltimore
    And cannas and white statuary.
I went home voluble and sore
    Influenced by Abraham and Mary.

II

At one the Apocalypse had spoken,
Von Moltke fell, I was housebroken.

At two how could I understand
The murder of Archduke Ferdinand?

France was involved with history,
I with my thumbs when I was three.

A sister came, we neared a war,
Paris was shelled when I was four.

I joined in our peach-kernel drive
For poison gas when I was five.

At six I cheered the big parade,
Burned sparklers and drank lemonade.

At seven I passed at school though I
Was far too young to say *Versailles*.

At eight the boom began to tire,
I tried to set our house on fire.

The Bolsheviks had drawn the line,
Lenin was stricken, I was nine.

— What evils do not retrograde
To my first odious decade?

III
Saints by whose pages I would swear,
    My Zarathustra, Edward Lear,
Ulysses, Werther, fierce Flaubert,
    Where are my books of yesteryear?

Sixteen and sixty are a pair;
    We twice live by philosophies;
My marginalia of the hair,
    Are you at one with Socrates?

Thirty subsides yet does not dare,
    Sixteen and sixty bang their fists.
How is it that I no longer care
    For Kant and the Transcendentalists?

Public libraries lead to prayer,
    EN APXH ἦν ὁ λόγος — still
Eliot and John are always there
    To tempt our admirari nil.

IV
I lived in a house of panels,
    Victorian, darkly made;
A virgin in bronze and marble
    Leered from the balustrade.

The street was a tomb of virtues,
    Autumnal for dreams and haunts;
I gazed from the polished windows
    Toward a neighborhood of aunts.

Mornings I practiced piano,
    Wrote elegies and sighed;
The evenings were conversations
    Of poetry and suicide.

Weltschmerz and mysticism,
    What tortures we undergo!
I loved with the love of Heinrich
    And the poison of Edgar Poe.

V

My first small book was nourished in the dark,
Secretly written, published, and inscribed.
Bound in wine-red, it made no brilliant mark.
Rather impossible relatives subscribed.

The best review was one I wrote myself
Under the name of a then-dearest friend.
Two hundred volumes stood upon my shelf
Saying my golden name from end to end.

I was not proud but seriously stirred;
Sorrow was song and money poetry's maid!
Sorrow I had in many a ponderous word,
But were the piper and the printer paid?

VI

The third-floor thoughts of discontented youth
Once saw the city, hardened against truth,
Get set for war. He coupled a last rime
And waited for the summons to end time.

It came. The box-like porch where he had sat,
The four bright boxes of a medium flat,
Chair he had sat in, glider where he lay
Reading the poets and prophets of his day,

He assigned abstractly to his dearest friend,
Glanced at the little street hooked at the end,
The line of poplars lately touched with spring,
Lovely as Laura, breathless, beckoning.

Mother was calm, until he left the door;
The trolley passed his sweetheart's house before
She was awake. The Armory was cold,
But naked, shivering, shocked he was enrolled.

It was the death he never quite forgot
Through the four years of death, and like as not
The true death of the best of all of us
Whose present life is largely posthumous.

VII

We waged a war within a war,
    A cause within a cause;
The glory of it was withheld
    In keeping with the laws
Whereby the public need not know
The pitfalls of the status quo.

Love was the reason for the blood:
    The black men of our land
Were seen to walk with pure white girls
    Laughing and hand in hand.
This most unreasonable state
No feeling White would tolerate.

We threw each other from the trams,
    We carried knives and pipes,
We sacrificed in self-defense
    Some of the baser types,
But though a certain number died
You would not call it fratricide.

The women with indignant tears
        Professed to love the Blacks,
And dark and wooly heads still met
        With heads of English flax.
Only the cockney could conceive
Of any marriage so naïve.

Yet scarcely fifty years before
        Their fathers rode to shoot
The undressed aborigines,
        Though not to persecute.
A fine distinction lies in that
They have no others to combat.

By order of the high command
        The black men were removed
To the interior and north;
        The crisis thus improved,
Even the women could detect
Their awful fall from intellect.

VIII

I plucked the bougainvillaea
        In Queensland in time of war;
The train stopped at the station
        And I reached it from my door.

I have never kept a flower
        And this one I never shall
I thought as I laid the blossom
        In the leaves of *Les Fleurs du Mal.*

I read my book in the desert
        In the time of death and fear,
The flower slipped from the pages
        And fell to my lap, my dear.

I sent it inside my letter,
        The purplest kiss I knew,
And thus you abused my passion
        With "A most Victorian Jew."

From
Poems 1940–1953
(1953)

Israel

When I think of the liberation of Palestine,
When my eye conceives the great black English line
Spanning the world news of two thousand years,
My heart leaps forward like a hungry dog,
My heart is thrown back on its tangled chain,
My soul is hangdog in a Western chair.

When I think of the battle for Zion I hear
The drop of chains, the starting forth of feet
And I remain chained in a Western chair.
My blood beats like a bird against a wall,
I feel the weight of prisons in my skull
Falling away; my forebears stare through stone.

When I see the name of Israel high in print
The fences crumble in my flesh; I sink
Deep in a Western chair and rest my soul.
I look the stranger clear to the blue depths
Of his unclouded eye. I say my name
Aloud for the first time unconsciously.

Speak of the tillage of a million heads
No more. Speak of the evil myth no more
Of one who harried Jesus on his way
Saying, *Go faster.* Speak no more
Of the yellow badge, *secta nefaria.*
Speak the name only of the living land.

The Minute

The office building treads the marble dark,
The mother-clock with wide and golden dial
Suffers and glows. Now is the hour of birth
Of the tremulous egg. Now is the time of correction.
O midnight, zero of eternity,
Soon on a million bureaus of the city
Will lie the new-born minute.

The new-born minute on the bureau lies,
Scratching the glass with infant kick, cutting
With diamond cry the crystal and expanse
Of timelessness. This pretty tick of death
Etches its name upon the air. I turn
Titanically in distant sleep, expelling
From my lungs the bitter gas of life.

The loathsome minute grows in length and strength,
Bending its spring to forge an iron hour
That rusts from link to link, the last one bright,
The late one dead. Between the shining works
Range the clean angels, studying that tick
Like a strange dirt, but will not pick it up
Nor move it gingerly out of harm's way.

An angel is stabbed and is carried aloft howling,
For devils have gathered on a ruby jewel
Like red mites on a berry; others arrive
To tend the points with oil and smooth the heat.
See how their vicious faces, lit with sweat,
Worship the train of wheels; see how they pull
The tape-worm Time from nothing into thing.

I with my distant heart lie wide awake
Smiling at that Swiss-perfect engine room
Driven by tiny evils. Knowing no harm
Even of gongs that loom and move in towers
And hands as high as iron masts, I sleep,
At which sad sign the angels in a flock
Rise and sweep past me, spinning threads of fear.

The Figurehead

Watching my paralytic friend
Caught in the giant clam of himself
Fast on the treacherous shoals of his bed,
I look away to the place he had left
Where at a decade's distance he appeared
To pause in his walk and think of a limp.
One day he arrived at the street bearing
The news that he dragged an ancient foot:
The people on their porches seemed to sway.

Though there are many wired together
In this world and the next, my friend
Strains in his clamps. He is all sprung
And locked in the rust of inner change.
The therapist who plucks him like a harp
Is a cold torture: the animal bleats
And whimpers on its far seashore
As she leans to her find with a smooth hunger.

Somewhere in a storm my pity went down:
It was a wooden figurehead
With sea-hard breasts and polished mouth.
But women wash my friend with brine
From shallow inlets of their eyes,
And women rock my friend with waves
That pulsate from the female moon.
They gather at his very edge and haul
My driftwood friend toward their fires.

Speaking of dancing, joking of sex,
I watch my paralytic friend
And seek my pity in those wastes where he
Becomes my bobbing figurehead.
Then as I take my leave I wade
Loudly into the shallows of his pain,
I splash like a vacationer,
I scare his legs and stir the time of day
With rosy clouds of sediment.

The Potomac

The thin Potomac scarcely moves
But to divide Virginia from today;
    Rider, whichever is your way
You go due south and neither South improves;
Not this, of fractured columns and queer rents
    And rags that charm the nationalist,
Not that, the axle of the continents,
Nor the thin sky that flows unprejudiced
This side and that, cleansing the poisoned breath.

    For Thomas died a Georgian death
And now the legion bones of Arlington
    Laid out in marble alphabets
Stare on the great tombs of the capitol
    Where heroes calcified and cool
    Ponder the soldier named Unknown
Whose lips are guarded with live bayonets.

    Yet he shall speak though sentries walk
And columns with their cold Corinthian stalk
    Shed gold-dust pollen on Brazil
    To turn the world to Roman chalk;
Yet he shall speak, yet he shall speak
    Whose sulphur lit the flood-lit Dome,
    Whose hands were never in the kill,
Whose will was furrows of Virginia loam.

But not like London blown apart by boys
Who learned the books of love in English schools,
His name shall strike the fluted columns down;
These shall lie buried deep as fifty Troys,
The money fade like leaves from green to brown,
And embassies dissolve to molecules.

Going to School

(Phi Beta Kappa poem, Harvard)

What shall I teach in the vivid afternoon
With the sun warming the blackboard and a slip
Of cloud catching my eye?
Only the cones and sections of the moon
Out of some flaking page of scholarship,
Only some foolish heresy
To counteract the authority of prose.
The ink runs freely and the dry chalk flows
Into the silent night of seven slates
Where I create the universe as if
It grew out of some old rabbinic glyph
Or hung upon the necessity of Yeats.

O dry imaginations, drink this dust
That grays the room and powders my coat sleeve,
For in this shaft of light
I dance upon the intellectual crust
Of our own age and hold this make-believe
Like holy-work before your sight.
This is the list of books that time has burned,
These are the lines that only poets have learned,
The frame of dreams, the symbols that dilate;
Yet when I turn from this dark exercise
I meet your bright and world-considering eyes
That build and build and never can create.

I gaze down on the garden with its green
Axial lines and scientific pond
And watch a man in white
Stiffly pursue a butterfly between
Square hedges where he takes it overhand
Into the pocket of his net.
Ah psyche, sinking in the bottled fumes,
Dragging your slow wings while the hunt resumes.
I say, "He placed an image on the pool
Of the Great Mind to float there like a leaf
And then sink downward to the dark belief
Of the Great Memory of the Hermetic School."

I say, "Linnaeus drowned the names of flowers
With the black garlands of his Latin words;
The gardens now are his,
The drug-bright blossoms of the glass are ours.
I think a million taxidermist's birds
Sing in the mind of Agassiz
Who still retained one image of the good,
Who said a fish is but a thought of God.
— This is the flat world circled by its dogs,
This is the right triangle held divine
Before bald Euclid drew his empty line
And shame fell on the ancient astrologues."

The eyes strike angles on the farther wall,
Divine geometry forms upon the page,
I feel a sense of shame.
Then as the great design begins to pall
A cock crows in a laboratory cage
And I proceed. "As for the name,
It is the potency itself of thing,
It is the power-of-rising of the wing;
Without it death and feathers, for neither reed
Of Solomon nor quill of Shakespeare's goose
Ever did more or less than to deduce
Letter from number in our ignorant creed."

And what if he who blessed these walls should walk
Invisibly in the room? — My conscience prates,
"The great biologist
Who read the universe in a piece of chalk
Said all knowledge is good, all learning waits,
And wrong hypotheses exist
To order knowledge and to set it right.
We burn, he said, that others may have light.
These are the penetralia of the school
Of the last century. Under a later sky
We call both saint and fool to prophesy
The second cycle brimming at the full."

Then the clock strikes and I erase the board,
Clearing the cosmos with a sweep of felt,
Voiding my mind as well.
Now that the blank of reason is restored
And they go talking of the crazy Celt
And ghosts that sipped his muscatel,
I must escape their laughter unaware
And sidle past the question on the stair
To gain my office. Is the image lost
That burned and shivered in the speculum
Or does it hover in the upper room?
Have I deceived the student or the ghost?

Here in the quiet of the book-built dark
Where masonry of volumes walls me in
I should expect to find,
Returning to me on a lower arc,
Some image bodying itself a skin,
Some object thinking forth a mind.
This search necessitates no closer look.
I close my desk and choose a modern book
And leave the building. Low, as to astound,
The sun stands with its body on the line
That separates us. Low, as to combine,
The sun touches its image to the ground.

From
Poems of a Jew
(1958)

The Alphabet

The letters of the Jews as strict as flames
Or little terrible flowers lean
Stubbornly upwards through the perfect ages,
Singing through solid stone the sacred names.
The letters of the Jews are black and clean
And lie in chain-line over Christian pages.
The chosen letters bristle like barbed wire
That hedge the flesh of man,
Twisting and tightening the book that warns.
These words, this burning bush, this flickering pyre
Unsacrifices the bled son of man
Yet plaits his crown of thorns.

Where go the tipsy idols of the Roman
Past synagogues of patient time,
Where go the sisters of the Gothic rose,
Where go the blue eyes of the Polish women
Past the almost natural crime,
Past the still speaking embers of ghettos,
There rise the tinder flowers of the Jews.
The letters of the Jews are dancing knives
That carve the heart of darkness seven ways.
These are the letters that all men refuse
And will refuse until the king arrives
And will refuse until the death of time
And all is rolled back in the book of days.

Messias

Alone in the darkling apartment the boy
Was reading poetry when the doorbell rang;
The sound sped to his ear and winged his joy,
The book leaped from his lap on broken wing.

Down the gilt stairwell then he peered
Where an old man of patriarchal race
Climbed in an eastern language with his beard
A black halo around his paper face.

His glasses spun with vision and his hat
Was thick with fur in the August afternoon;
His silk suit crackled heavily with light
And in his hand a rattling canister shone.

Bigger he grew and softer the root words
Of the hieratic language of his heart,
And faced the boy, who flung the entrance wide
And fled in terror from the nameless hurt.

Past every door like a dead thing he swam,
Past the entablatures of the kitchen walls,
Down the red ringing of the fire escape
Singing with sun, to the green grass he came,

Sickeningly green, leaving the man to lurch
Bewildered through the house and seat himself
In the sacrificial kitchen after his march,
To study the strange boxes on the shelf.

There mother found him mountainous and alone,
Mumbling some singsong in a monotone,
Crumbling breadcrumbs in his scholar's hand
That wanted a donation for the Holy Land.

The Confirmation

When mothers weep and fathers richly proud
Worship on Sunday morning their tall son
And girls in white like angels in a play
  Tiptoe between the potted palms
  And all the crimson windows pray,
    The preacher bound in black
Opens his hands like pages of a book
  And holds the black and crimson law
  For every boy to look.

Last night between the chapters of a dream,
The photograph still sinning in the drawer,
The boy awoke; the moon shone in the yard
  On hairy hollyhocks erect
  And buds of roses pink and hard
    And on the solid wall
A square of light like movies fell to pose
  An actress naked in the night
    As hollyhock and rose.

And to confirm his sex, breathless and white
With benediction self-bestowed he knelt
Oh tightly married to his childish grip,
  And unction smooth as holy-oil
  Fell from the vessel's level lip
    Upon the altar-cloth;
Like Easter boys the blood sang in his head
  And all night long the tallow beads
    Like tears dried in the bed.

Come from the church, you parents and you girls,
And walk with kisses and with happy jokes
Beside this man. Be doubly proud, you priest,
    Once for his passion in the rose,
    Once for his body self-released;
        And speak aloud of her
Who in the perfect consciousness of joy
    Stood naked in the electric light
    And woke the hidden boy.

The First Time

Behind shut doors, in shadowy quarantine,
There shines the lamp of iodine and rose
That stains all love with its medicinal bloom.
This boy, who is no more than seventeen,
Not knowing what to do, takes off his clothes
As one might in a doctor's anteroom.

Then in a cross-draft of fear and shame
Feels love hysterically burn away,
A candle swimming down to nothingness
Put out by its own wetted gusts of flame,
And he stands smooth as uncarved ivory
Heavily curved for some expert caress.

And finally sees the always open door
That is invisible till the time has come,
And half falls through as through a rotten wall
To where chairs twist with dragons from the floor
And the great bed drugged with its own perfume
Spreads its carnivorous flower-mouth for all.

The girl is sitting with her back to him;
She wears a black thing and she rakes her hair,
Hauling her round face upward like moonrise;
She is younger than he, her angled arms are slim
And like a country girl her feet are bare.
She watches him behind her with old eyes,

Transfixing him in space like some grotesque,
Far, far from her where he is still alone
And being here is more and more untrue.
Then she turns round, as one turns at a desk,
And looks at him, too naked and too soon,
And almost gently asks: *Are you a Jew?*

The Murder of Moses

By reason of despair we set forth behind you
And followed the pillar of fire like a doubt,
To hold to belief wanted a sign,
Called the miracle of the staff and the plagues
Natural phenomena.

We questioned the expediency of the march,
Gossiped about you. What was escape
To the fear of going forward and Pharaoh's wheels?
When the chariots mired and the army flooded
Our cry of horror was one with theirs.

You always went alone, a little ahead,
Prophecy disturbed you, you were not a fanatic.
The women said you were meek, the men
Regarded you as a typical leader.
You and your black wife might have been foreigners.

We even discussed your parentage; were you really a Jew?
We remembered how Joseph had made himself a prince,
All of us shared in the recognition
Of his skill of management, sense of propriety,
Devotion to his brothers and Israel.

We hated you daily. Our children died. The water spilled.
It was as if you were trying to lose us one by one.
Our wandering seemed the wandering of your mind,
The cloud believed we were tireless,
We expressed our contempt and our boredom openly.

At last you ascended the rock; at last returned.
Your anger that day was probably His.
When we saw you come down from the mountain, your skin alight
And the stones of our law flashing,
We fled like animals and the dancers scattered.

We watched where you overturned the calf on the fire,
We hid when you broke the tablets on the rock,
We wept when we drank the mixture of gold and water.
We had hoped you were lost or had left us.
This was the day of our greatest defilement.

You were simple of heart; you were sorry for Miriam,
You reasoned with Aaron, who was your enemy.
However often you cheered us with songs and prayers
We cursed you again. The serpent bit us,
And mouth to mouth you entreated the Lord for our sake.

At the end of it all we gave you the gift of death.
Invasion and generalship were spared you.
The hand of our direction, resignedly you fell,
And while officers prepared for the river-crossing
The Old God blessed you and covered you with earth.

Though you were mortal and once committed murder
You assumed the burden of the covenant,
Spoke for the world and for our understanding.
Converse with God made you a thinker,
Taught us all early justice, made us a race.

From
The Bourgeois Poet
(1964)

Solipsism

The world is my dream, says the wise child, ever so wise, not stepping on
lines. I am the world, says the wise-eyed child. I made you, mother.
I made you, sky. Take care or I'll put you back in my dream.

If I look at the sun the sun will explode, says the wicked boy. If I look
at the moon I'll drain away. Where I stay I hold them in their places.
Don't ask me what I'm doing.

The simple son was sent to science college. There he learned how everything
worked.

The one who says nothing is told everything (not that he cares). The one
who dreamed me hasn't put me back. The sun and the moon, they
rise on time. I still don't know how the engine works; I can splice a
wire. That's about it.

The dream is my world, says the sick child. I am pure as these bed sheets.
(He writes fatigue on the vast expanses.) I'm in your dream, says the
wicked boy. The simple son has been decorated for objectivity. He
who says nothing is still being told.

De Sade looks down through the bars of the Bastille. They have stepped up
the slaughter of nobles.

The Bourgeois Poet

The bourgeois poet closes the door of his study and lights his pipe. Why am I in this box, he says to himself (although it is exactly as he planned). The bourgeois poet sits down at his inoffensive desk — a door with legs, a door turned table — and almost approves the careful disarray of books, papers, magazines and such artifacts as thumbtacks. The bourgeois poet is already out of matches and gets up. It is too early in the morning for any definite emotion and the B.P. smokes. It is beautiful in the midlands: green fields and tawny fields, sorghum the color of red morocco bindings, distant new neighborhoods, cleanly and treeless, and the Veterans Hospital fronted with a shimmering Indian Summer tree. The Beep feels seasonal, placid as a melon, neat as a child's football lying under the tree, waiting for whose hands to pick it up.

The Living Rooms of
My Neighbors

The living rooms of my neighbors are like beauty parlors, like night-club
powder rooms, like international airport first-class lounges. The bath-
rooms of my neighbors are like love nests — Dufy prints, black
Kleenex, furry towels, toilets so highly bred they fill and fall without
a sigh (why is there no bidet in so-clean America?). The kitchens of
my neighbors are like cars: what gleaming dials, what toothy en-
amels, engines that click and purr, idling the hours away. The base-
ments of my neighbors are like kitchens; you could eat off the floor.
Look at the furnace, spotless as a breakfront, standing alone, prize
piece, the god of the household.

But I'm no different. I arrange my books with a view to their appearance.
Some highbrow titles are prominently displayed. The desk in my study
is carefully littered; after some thought I hang a diploma on the wall,
only to take it down again. I sit at the window where I can be seen.
What do my neighbors think of me — I hope they think of me. I fix
the light to hit the books. I lean some rows one way, some rows
another.

A man's house is his stage. Others walk on to play their bit parts. Now and
again a soliloquy, a birth, an adultery.

The bars of my neighbors are various, ranging from none at all to the
nearly professional, leather stools, automatic coolers, a naked
painting, a spittoon for show.
The businessman, the air-force captain, the professor with tenure — it's a
neighborhood with a sky.

The Wood

Wood for the fireplace, wood for the floor, what is the life span? Sometimes before I lay the log on the fire I think: it's sculpture wood, it's walnut. Maybe someone would find a figure in it, as children find faces in the open fire (I never have). Then I lay it on the flames like a heretic, where it pauses a moment, then joins in the singing. There's oak in this cord too. My floor is oak. I watched them lay this floor, for a vastly slower fire. The grooved pieces are fitted together; it's more like a game than work; there are many choices. The grain falls arbitrarily, dark streaks and light, dots and dashes, swirls and striped shields.

Dead wood can last forever (is it dead)? Dead wood glows in palaces, rosy and dark as masterpieces. I worship wood, split my own logs in the driveway, using a maul and iron wedges. The cracking-apart is hard and sweet. I touch wood for my superstition, using five fingers as an extra precaution. My gods would all be wood if I had gods, not stone or gold or Peter's smooth-kissed toe.

In woodless Italy houses are built without a sound, no ring of hammer on nail or wood. All is quiet, stone laid upon stone, rubble, cement, tufa, travertine, tile. Rarely you see some show-off house of wood, exotic among the blinding stucco, soft among the cool and stony facings, the marbly infinitude.

The Clearing

In the Clearing I am at peace. Place without memory or charm. Stores practically empty of goods, schools kindly and frightened. This Clearing is a beach without a sea.

Here there is only sporadic and symbolic violence. The clouds are all the news. Each tree is grown by hand.

By degrees, those who have ambience are alienated from the Dark Towers: the German groaning for the picture galleries; the bank director who bakes his own bread; the housewife with a flair for words who has given up bathing; the itinerant pianist with ice-blue eyes; the Siberian physicist with his smug compliments; the Oxford don with the dirtiest stories; the rabbi with the mystique of the Sabbath Queen; the bearded classicist with broken arches; the veteran bomber of three world wars. I talk to the man who brings the firewood. He gives me a wedge for a present.

The citizens of Nowhere scatter in all directions.

Upon my discharge from the Army my handwriting changed. Neat slant characters gave way to square and upright. The color of the ink no longer mattered. I met a poet who printed all his words. (I thought this dangerous.) I find I can barely read the mail that comes. Sometimes I have it read to me. I tend to misunderstand the words. My answers are brief. I still wait for the mailman, a vestigial pleasure. Mail in the Clearing is lighter.

Hair

One by one my troops desert. A hair at a time. One by one and there is no return. Yesterday it was dark and soft, unnoticeable as a pore. Today it sticks up at a crazy angle, bristling with what act of rebellion. Yesterday a tendril, a decoration, a vestige of biology, today barbed wire. I count them all till I've lost count. I count from the top of my head. The revolution started in that sector.

In the sole world of the self that is how it happens. One cell revolts against the general harmony. The body's bourgeois security is threatened. The government gives a perceptible shudder. One cell alone goes off, giving the finger sign of obscenity. Urchins and panhandlers cheer him on. In a moment he is making speeches. Then the police, then the militia, soon the victorious grave.

Rising crooked on my arm, darting wickedly out of my eyebrows, blanching my chest like sun, what do you want, blackmailers, professional mourners. I see you starting down my arms like lice, infiltrating to the very wrist. How far will you go? When will order be restored. Halfway measures for fops and actors, black dye, tweezers, cuticle scissors. Shall I give you away? I know your little game. I saw it in the bath the other day. This plot would tickle Rabelais. A pubic hair turned silver gray!

Beautiful Thing

Autumn reminds me that you bit my lips, excellent nurse of the most famous hospital, with puffy eyes and advertisable rear. North of beautiful Baltimore, in valley taverns, reminiscent of imagined England, we watched from the rail fence the blessing of hounds. At the place of our date you made a pass at my just-married friend in the face of his bride. She is dark and full, a Renoir woman with Brooklyn accent. You are light and thin, lacking in humor or observation. How slowly the dark one moves while you engage her husband in jokes and hugs and public thigh-pushes, all thoroughly insincere. Till the bride's laughter congeals in her throat and suddenly she is flying hands and knives of fingernails slashing wickedly at your soft attractive face, your sleepless eyes with albino lashes.

At night in the improvised bed by the living-room fire in the stone cottage you bite and use your nails. Afterwards you want me to stay inside you the entire night, even asleep. I laugh, I beg. Instead of whispering *darling* you whisper (with such conviction) *you worm!*

Office Love

Office love, love of money and fight, love of calculated sex. The offices reek with thin volcanic metal. Tears fall in typewriters like drops of solder. Brimstone of brassieres, low voices, the whirr of dead-serious play. From the tropical tree and the Rothko in the Board Room to the ungrammatical broom closet fragrant with waxes, to the vast typing pool where coffee is being served by dainty waitresses maneuvering their hand trucks, music almost unnoticeable falls. The very telephones are hard and kissable, the electric water cooler sweetly sweats. Gold simmers to a boil in braceleted and sunburned cheeks. What ritual politeness nevertheless, what subtlety of clothing. And if glances meet, if shoulders graze, there's no harm done. Flowers, celebrations, pregnancy leave, how the little diamonds sparkle under the psychologically soft-colored ceilings. It's an elegant windowless world of soft pressures and efficiency joys, of civilized mishaps — mere runs in the stocking, papercuts.

Where the big boys sit the language is rougher. Phone calls to China and a private shower. No paper visible anywhere. Policy is decided by word of mouth like gangsters. There the power lies and is sexless.

High School

Waiting in front of the columnar high school (the old ones look like banks, or rather insurance companies) I glance over the top of my book. The bells go off like slow burglar alarms; innumerable sixteeners saunter out. There's no running as in the lower schools, none of that helpless gaiety of the small. Here comes a surly defiance. As in a ritual, each lights a cigaret just at the boundary where the tabu ends. Each chews. The ones in cars rev up their motors and have bad complexions like gangsters. The sixteeners are all playing gangster.

The sea of subjectivity comes at you like a tidal wave, splashing the cuffs of middle-aged monuments. War is written on their unwritten faces. They try out wet dreams and wandering mind. They're rubbing Aladdin's lamp in the locker room. They pray for moments of objectivity as drunkards pray for the one that puts you out. They've captured the telephone centers, the microphones, the magazine syndicates (they've left the movies to us). I wait behind the wheel and spy; it's enemy territory all right. My daughter comes, grows taller as she approaches. It's a moment of panic.

But once at night in the sweet and sour fall I dropped her off at the football game. The bowl of light lit up the creamy Corinthian columns. A cheer went up from the field so shrill, so young, like a thousand birds in a single cage, like a massacre of child-brides in a clearing, I felt ashamed and grave. The horror of their years stoned me to death.

The Child Who Is Silent

The child who is silent stands against his father, lovingly looking up at him as if to say without a trace of defiance: I will speak when I have decided. He marches around the table smiling intelligently, now and then deigning to say something, perhaps "locomotive." It is somewhat frightening, a kind of rebuff to grownups. The doctors smile and shrug. If the parents are worried they don't display it. It's only like living in the last house at the edge of the subdivision. There's a bit of farm left and a highway beyond: if someone should rattle the back door in the night . . . There is a child of two minds who says nothing and who is drinking it all in. Obviously happy, very much loved, handsome and straight, laughing and playing, withholding that gift we all abuse. In that room is a tower of books with their backs to us, eloquently quiet too. Man is a torrent of language, even in death. But visitors use longer words. The little philosopher goes about his business.

This is the town where the railroads ended, the wagon trains formed in the dry gray grass. It's this frontier of speech we are always crossing. The locomotive is ridiculously dying, lumbering off to the deep clay pits to settle among the mastodon bones. The piano is thinking of Mozart. On the very top, legs crossed, at ease, sits the blue-eyed boy who holds his peace.

Generations

The look of shock on an old friend's face after years of not meeting, as if perhaps we were in a play, dressed for one of the final acts. The make-up of the years (infant, schoolboy, lover, soldier, judge of others, patriarch and ultimate old child) is on us. Those who remain the same and those who change their jaws. One has milky moons around the eyes or knotty knuckles. Many and varied are the studies in gray. The spectrum of whites amazes.

A generation moves in stateliness. It arrives like a pageant and passes down the street. The children sit on the curbs and watch. There are dignitaries and clowns, the men with medals and the cross-carriers. The owners walk abreast for the afternoon: they carry the banner which reads: the business of the world is — business. Manacled dictators walk alone through the crowded silence: four swordsmen guard them like points of the compass. The poets arrive on burros, bumping each other. Theologians packed in a hearse peer out like sickly popes. A phalanx of technologists singing the latest love songs in marching rhythms. Movie stars escorting diplomats (it's hard to tell them apart).

Nine of the greatest novelists, of ridiculous difference in height and girth. Two modern saints on litters. The generation proceeds to the cenotaph, the only common meeting place. In side streets the coming generation, not even looking, waits its turn and practices a new and secret language. (They think it's secret: that's what's so depressing.) Their hero is also gray and still in high school. He drives a hundred miles an hour into a tree.

I Am an Atheist Who Says His Prayers

I am an atheist who says his prayers.

I am an anarchist, and a full professor at that. I take the loyalty oath.

I am a deviate. I fondle and contribute, backscuttle and brown, father of three.

I stand high in the community. My name is in *Who's Who*. People argue about my modesty.

I drink my share and yours and never have enough. I free-load officially and unofficially.

A physical coward, I take on all intellectuals, established poets, popes, rabbis, chiefs of staff.

I am a mystic. I will take an oath that I have seen the Virgin. Under the dry pandanus, to the scratching of kangaroo rats, I achieve psychic onanism. My tree of nerves electrocutes itself.

I uphold the image of America and force my luck. I write my own ticket to oblivion.

I am of the race wrecked by success. The audience brings me news of my death. I write out of boredom, despise solemnity. The wrong reason is good enough for me.

I am of the race of the prematurely desperate. In poverty of comfort I lay gunpowder plots. I lapse my insurance.

I am the Babbitt metal of the future. I never read more than half of a book. But that half I read forever.

I love the palimpsest, statues without heads, fertility dolls of the continent of Mu. I dream prehistory, the invention of dye. The palms of the dancers' hands are vermillion. Their heads oscillate like the cobra. High-caste woman smelling of earth and silk, you can dry my feet with your hair.

I take my place beside the Philistine and unfold my napkin. This afternoon I defend the Marines. I goggle at long cars.

Without compassion I attack the insane. Give them the horsewhip!

The homosexual lectures me brilliantly in the beer booth. I can feel my muscles soften. He smiles at my terror.

Pitchpots flicker in the lemon groves. I gaze down on the plains of Hollywood. My fine tan and my arrogance, my gray hair and my sneakers, O Israel!

Wherever I am I become. The power of entry is with me. In the doctor's office a patient, calm and humiliated. In the foreign movies a native, shabby enough. In the art gallery a person of authority (there's a secret way of approaching a picture. Others move off). The high official insults me to my face. I say nothing and accept the job. He offers me whiskey.

How beautifully I fake! I convince myself with men's room jokes and epigrams. I paint myself into a corner and escape on pulleys of the unknown. Whatever I think at the moment is true. Turn me around in my tracks; I will take your side.

For the rest, I improvise and am not spiteful and water the plants on the cocktail table.

My Century

All things remain to be simplified. I find I must break free
of the poetry trap.

The books I hunger for all always out, never to be returned:
illuminations, personal bibles, diatribes, chapters denied
acceptance in scripture, Tobit blinded by sparrows
muting warm dung in his eyes, immense declarations
of revolt, manuals of the practice of love.

I seek the entrance of the rabbit hole. Maybe it's the door
that has no name.

My century, take savagery to your heart. Take wooden idols,
walk them through the streets. Bow down to Science.

My century that boils history to a pulp for newspaper, my
century of the million-dollar portrait, century of the
decipherment of Linear B and the old scrolls, century
of the dream of penultimate man (he wanders among
the abandoned skyscrapers of Kansas; he has already
forgotten language), century of the turning-point of
time, the human wolf pack and the killing light.

Amsterdam Whores

Each in her well-lighted picture window, reading a book or magazine, the Amsterdam whores look quite domestic. The canals, as picturesque as expected, add their serenity. The customers stroll from window to window, back and forth, comparing merchandise. Where a curtain is drawn, business is being transacted. These are big, fine, strapping whores, heavy in the leg, blond, as is the preference. They don't display their wares, no more than crossing a leg. It's like a picture gallery, Flemish School, silent through varnish and glaze. What detail, what realism of texture, what narrative! And look at this master-piece:

A solid blond sits in her window at an angle. She appears to be looking out, expressionless. Just back of her stands an African king in round white hat and lengthy white embroidered robe of satin, it may be. Behind him stands his servant, very straight. The king's face is a thin and noble ebony. And without looking at either African the whore holds one hand back of her shoulder, feeling the robe of the African king with eloquent fingers, weighing the heft of the silk in her thoughtful hand.

Jazz

August Saturday night on the Negro street the trolleys clang and break sweet
dusty smoke. Cars hoot meaningless signals. The air is in a sweat of
Jim Crow gaiety, shopping, milling, rubbing of flesh, five miles of
laughter in white Baltimore. The second floor dance hall has a fa-
mous trumpet. You can't move on the floor, which rolls like waves
and is in actual danger of giving way. The temperature adds to the
frenzy. There is no pause in the jump and scream of the jazz, heat
waves of laughter, untranslatable slang. The dancing is demonic,
terpsichorean. It's like a war of pleasure. It's the joy of work. The
fatigue is its own reward.

Across the street in the corner drug store where whiskey is sold and every
blandishment of skin, a teeming Negress crowds at the perfume
counter, big arms like haunches and bosom practically bare. She
laughs with her friends above the cut-glass bottles with Frenchified
names and recently invented colors. She purchases a sizable vial of
some green scent, pays green dry money, unstoppers the bottle and
dumps the entire load between her breasts! O glorious act of laughter
in the half-serious bazaar of the Jew-store!

Nebraska

I love Nowhere where the factories die of malnutrition.

I love Nowhere where there are no roads, no rivers, no interesting Indians,

Where history is invented in the History Department and there are no centennials of anything.

Where every tree is planted by hand and has a private tutor.

Where the "parts" have to be ordered and the sky settles all questions,

Where travelers from California bitch at the backwardness and New Yorkers step on the gas in a panic,

Where the grass in winter is gray not brown,

Where the population diminishes.

Here on the boundary of the hired West, equidistant from every tourist office, and the air is washed by distance, here at last there is nothing to recommend.

May no one ever attempt a recommendation; Chicago be as far as Karachi.

Though the warriors come with rockets, may they fall off the trucks.

May the voting be light and the clouds like a cruise and the criminal boredom enter the district of hogs.

I love Nowhere where the human brag is a brag of neither time nor place,

But an elephant house of Smithsonian bones and the white cathedrals of grain,

The feeding-lots in the snow with the steers huddled in symmetrical misery, backs to the sleet,

To beef us up in the Beef State plains, something to look at.

The Cracking-Plant

From the top floor of the Tulsa hotel I gaze at the night beauty of the cracking-plant. Candlelit city of small gas flames by the thousands, what a lovely anachronism dancing below like an adolescent's dream of the 1880s, the holy gas redeemed from Baudelaire's mustachioed curses. Elsewhere are the white lights of the age, but here, like a millionaire who frowns on electricity, the opulence of flame. Descending on Rome from the air at night, a similar beauty: the weak Italian bulbs like faulty rheostats yellowly outline the baroque curves of the Tiber, the semicircles of the monstrous Vatican, endless broken parabolas.

The cracking-plant is equally palatial. Those oil men in the silent elevator, like princes with their voices of natural volume, their soft hats and their name-drops (like balloons of words in the mouths of caricatures in political cartoons), men of many mansions. The doors of the room are mahogany. Through one which adjoins and is locked I hear the guttural laughter of undress, neither leisurely nor quick, indistinct wording, and all is silent but a woman's moan. Now it rises like the grip of pain; it is almost loud; it is certainly sincere, like the pent-up grief of deep relief; now it is round, now vibrant, now it is scaly as it grows. (Then it steps off into nothingness.)

I stand awed in my stocking-feet and move respectfully toward the window, as a man in an art gallery moves toward a more distant masterpiece to avoid the musical chatter of intruders. The cracking-plant sails on through the delicate Oklahoma night, flying the thousand hot flags of Laputa.

Burlesk

Hart Crane, though handicapped, did well with the burlesk: all but her belly
buried in the floor. Magdalene? Perhaps. In Kansas City I pay my
respects to the dying art. The theater is in ruins, the ticket-taker
only half-conscious. Wine took him long ago. The carpet in the aisle
is ripped; twice I snag my foot. The rank air smells of disinfectant.
All seats are vacant except the first two rows. These are lit up as
in a Rembrandt picture, the glowing center of the operation. I sit
down inches from the drum. It lifts my hair each second it is
smashed. The snare drum hisses and the block clicks. The cymbal
crazes.

She's halfway through, already down to the sash that hangs like a silk
muffler between her buttocks. She gyrates with an expert beat, more
round than sharp. Small-breasted, her nipples glitter with stardust —
some local ordinance. She is very pretty, not what you would ex-
pect, almost indifferently dancing her career. Cold flows from her
steady limbs; stately she spreads her thighs for the climactic grind,
when at the highest throw she slips her final string, holding one
hand over the part like a live fig leaf, and flittering her fingers off
— and we are there, and she is all but hairless.

Our faces light up with intelligence.

Bouquet

All tropic places smell of mold. A letter from Karachi smells of mold. A book I had in New Guinea twenty years ago smells of mold. Cities in India smell of mold and dung. After a while you begin to like it. The curry dishes in the fine Bombay restaurant add the dung flavor. In the villages dung patties plastered to the walls, the leaving of the cows the only cooking fuel. The smell rubs into the blood.

Paris in the winter smells of wood smoke and fruit. Near the Gare St. Lazare in the freezing dusk the crowds pour slowly down the streets in every direction. A police van the size of a Pullman car goes at a walking pace. The gendarme keeps jumping down from the rear like a streetcar conductor in the old days. He is examining identity cards of pedestrians, especially the females. A girl comes swinging along, her pocketbook in rhythm with her behind. She is bareheaded and wears a raincoat. The gendarme examines her identity card. She is motioned into the paddy wagon.

Salzburg, the castle smells of snow and peat. Baltimore, old oaken bucket. Portsmouth, Virginia, roses and diesel oil. Dublin, coal dust, saccharine whiskey, bitter bodies. Damp gusts of Siena doorways. Warehouses of Papeete, acrid smell of copra, frangipani, saltwater and mold. Smell of rotting water in Hollandia.

Unbreathable jungles, parks subtle and cool. Backstage the ballet dancers wipe their sweat; "the entire stage stinks like a stable." Sewer gas of beauty parlors. Electric smell of hair in rut. Talcum powder, earliest recollection. Rome, the armpit of the universe.

Fox Hole

Quintana lay in the shallow grave of coral. The guns boomed stupidly fifty yards away. The plasma trickled into his arm. Naked and filthy, covered with mosquitoes, he looked at me as I read his white cloth tag. How do you feel, Quintana? He looks away from my gaze. I lie: we'll get you out of here sometime today.

I never saw him again, dead or alive. Skin and bones, with eyes as soft as soot, neck long as a thigh, a cross on his breastbone not far from the dog tags. El Greco was all I could think of. Quintana lying in his shallow foxhole waiting to be evacuated. A dying man with a Spanish name equals El Greco. A truck driver from Dallas probably.

When the Japs were making the banzai charge, to add insult to death, they came at us screaming the supreme insult: *Babe Ruth, go to hell!* The Americans, on the other hand, when the Japs flew over dropping sticks of explosives, shouted into the air, as if they could hear: *Tojo, eat shit!*

Soldiers fall in love with the enemy all too easily. It's the allies they hate. Every war is its own excuse. That's why they're all surrounded with ideals. That's why they're all crusades.

The Nature of Belief

When suffering is everywhere, that is of the nature of belief. When the leaders are corrupted, Pope or Commissar, nor do the people flicker an eyelash, that is of the nature of belief. When there are anniversaries of battle or martyrdom, that is of the nature of belief. When there is the slogan Credo quia absurdum or intellectual proof of the existence of God, that is of the nature of belief. When priests pray for victory and generals invoke heaven, when prisons fill with children, that is of the nature of belief. When the word *evil* appears in newspapers, *moral* in the mouths of policemen, *culture* in the prepared speeches of politicians, all that is of the nature of belief. Belief makes blood flow. Belief infects the dead with more belief. Now it flows in our veins. Now it floats in the clouds.

French Poetry

French poetry that always goes itself one better.

French poetry of figure 5's and rust carnations.

French poetry of the tongue that tastes of women and children, spatulas and rubber plants.

French poetry of the tiniest print to be read with bifocals when snow first enters the rain with its wicked announcements of defeat.

French poetry of marginal headaches, wood fires, cold, sixteen-millimeter surrealist films, Martinique jazz and the woman across the way, utmost gravity and indestructible balance, winner of the double medallion,

Easter Island images, the monstrous solemnity of patriotic children and ribbons.

French poetry of convenience, Satanism, baroque brass keys to hospitals, and cats.

French poetry of the line drawn with the fist on the pale nuance,

Overly cultivated snows, sick castles.

French poetry of the exquisite ruins of conversation.

French poetry that upsets the stomach of the future.

Of frockless priests, glorious geometricians, child insurrectionists.

French poetry of the Statue of Liberty, battered by kisses and dentists,

Ropy veins of the feet of matrons and whores, stigmata, épée.

French poetry of the Missouri River, the Platte, Yarra, gutter water of the rue Jacob.

Gloire, Vrai, et cetera.

Baudelaire in Iowa

They held a celebration for you, Charles, in Iowa. I was asked but I
regretted. It was the hundredth birthday of your book, your proper
Christian book called *Flowers of Evil*. (Or is it THE *Flowers of Evil?*
I never know.) And in that hymnal, how well you made yourself in
the image of Poe — Poe with a cross, that's what you are, adored
of the gangster age. In fact, aren't you a children's poet? Aren't you
the Lewis Carroll of small vice? Your shabby Wonderland of pus and
giant nipple, your cats and jewels and cheap perfumes, your licking
Lesbians and make-believe Black Mass, O purulence of Original Sin.
And always playing it safe in the end, like Disneyland. So many safety
devices, pulleys, cranks, classical Alexandrines. It's Iowa for you,
restless spirit, where elderly ladies embezzle millions in the *acte
gratuite*. You'll need no naturalization papers here. And yet I loved
you once, and Delacroix and Berlioz — all in my gangster age. The
little boy in me loved you all, O solemn Charles, so photogenic. And
this is my flower for your anniversary. I fashioned it of Mexican tin
and black nail polish, little French Swinburne burning in Iowa City.

Randall Jarrell

Randall, I like your poetry terribly, yet I'm afraid to say so. Not that my praise keeps you awake — though I'm afraid it does. I can't help liking them. I even like the whine, the make-believe whiplash with the actual wire in it. Once when you reviewed me badly (you must) I wrote you: "I felt as if I had been run over but not hurt." That made you laugh. I was happy. It wasn't much of a triumph but it worked. When people ask about you I am inclined to say: He's an assassin (a word I never use). I'm inclined to say: Why are you always yourself? Your love of Rilke — if it's love — your intimacy with German and God knows what all, your tenderness and terrorization, your prose sentences — like Bernini graves, staggeringly expensive, Italianate, warm, sentences once-and-for-all. And the verses you leave half-finished in mid-air — I once knew a woman who never finished a sentence. Your mind is always at its best, your craft the finest craft "money can buy" you would say with a barb. I'm afraid of you. Who wouldn't be. But I rush to read you, whatever you print. That's news.

Clowning

Dylan wasn't dapper. Uncle Saul was a dandy. Dylan stole and borrowed. Uncle Saul likewise. Dylan stole a shirt or two and some bottles of whiskey. Uncle Saul purloined whole wardrobes, used checking accounts that didn't belong to him, charged at the best shops under others' names. Dylan wore motley, Uncle Saul silk. Dylan was short and curly. Uncle Saul wore Cuban heels to raise himself and ordered Scotch in the barber's chair. Dylan played at pinballs. Uncle won the monthly rent at poker or bridge. Dylan borrowed women. Uncle Saul hired them and kept them in love nests. Dylan's look was straight and far into your eyes. The eyes of Uncle Saul were always merry and shrewd but you couldn't see beyond their twinkle and scheme. Dylan was a civilian. Uncle wangled a commission in the Army, only to be discharged for juggling money records. Uncle Saul kept the table choking with laughter and sang falsetto and clowned in a lavender dressing gown, with masses of hair on his chest. Dylan toured America like a favorite nephew, sprinkling dynamite on the nipples of female professors. He had the discipline of a lovely knave.

Now both are dead, Dylan and Uncle Saul. Dylan was taken by the pickling of his beautiful brain. The sacred oxygen could not reach the convolutions. Uncle Saul was taken thrice by the heart, thrice by the broken personality. Uncle Saul joked in the lobby of the plush nuthouse, wearing a brilliant sportcoat and shined elegant shoes. The black hair dye had vanished; his hair was snowy white. They gave him the shock treatment until his heart exploded. Dylan lay inert with the Moses bumps on his forehead amidst the screaming of wives and the groans of lovers and drinkers. And the Beat said — iambic killed him.

Roethke

Glottal as a bottle, everybody loves you, only you don't believe it. Hulk of greenery among the desert great, your roots grab continents of sham and groan. You masticate all dictionaries and spew out one-word spitballs on the walls. You blackboard buccaneers of blah. You housel planetaria of spurt. You shoeshine flesh with hail and hurt. Psychologically, you sport.

The music flutes: you're nursing Mother Goose. You know her nasty secrets like a name (dirty old woman stinking of gin). Have you found the pickled foetuses! Does your poem purl in Polish? Who's bigger than you — those squishy dreams?

The decencies file in: such pretty girls, such beardy boys. Your rhythms that throb like ocean motors.

Now and then the darkness of stanzas. That bridge of ice-capped sawtooth monuments bites at the sky like industrial diamonds. You grit your teeth on broken glass, sing with a geographical tongue on the sly nights of Seattle. Art is a blood pudding foreign as frescoes. Where you dig down we are, we are. Under the smoky glass we are. How the flukes splash, ha-ha, baby!

Poets' Corner

As richly documented as the hell of priests, yes, there is a hell, the hell of sick poets, the hell of history. Those in whom honesty has turned to policy. Those diseased by notice. Those who invent new prosodies, with a logical or graphic notation. Those who wear the cold hand-cuffs of rhyme. Those who construct a religion of the beautiful, with symbols as the means and myth as the end. Those who mistake rage for intensity, symmetry for design, metaphor for focus, drunkenness for vision. Those who make an example of their lives and who commit acts of personal violence for public response. These inhabit the hell of poets.

Some die early by disease or accident. Some jump in the sea or drink lacerating poisons manufactured for toilets. Some lie in asylums with eyeballs metamorphosed to marble. (You cannot penetrate below their surface.) Some fall on their knees before two pieces of wood or a stone belly. Some join the revolutions and are gladly shot. Some become officials, laureates, men of affairs or major diplomats. Some become abstractionists, actuaries, mathematicians. Some become salesmen or lay priests, after their voluptuous poems are in print. Some become preachers in the last half of their lives, constructing faultless sermons. Some succumb to pageantry, some to algolagnia.

Glad Hand

I'm writing this poem for someone to see when I'm not looking. This is an open book. I want to be careful to startle you gently. The poem is about your looking at it, as one looks at a woman covertly. (I wonder what she's doing in this town; it's a long way from the look in her eyes.) The rings of my big notebook stand open like the rib cage of a barracuda. Careful with your fingers.

I'm writing this poem for an after-dinner friend who's using my pipe tobacco or my pen. I'd like some phrase to catch his eye. I'd like some phrase to wake him up in the early hours, as one wakes up with a fragment of a tune in his head (the melody for the day). The toilet bowls glow graciously and there's a box of the best Kleenex on the sink. I'm writing this poem for hospitality. I can't stand people who say Help Yourself. That always means Don't Be a Pig. Tired of picking the locks of poems I leave this one for all and sundry. To put your name in it would be a dirty trick.

Younger I dreamed of being a poet whose trash basket was rifled by scholars. I learned to write trash-basket poems. But this is closer to my real desire. I'm writing this poem as much for you as a poem is possible. It stands there like a half-filled glass, both coming and going. I'm a bad host. The drinks are too strong; I don't know how to carve (I say with a grin, I'm left-handed). This is a poem to sneak at a glance. (I'm writing it to mean, not be.)

Fame

What kind of notation is in my *Time* file for my life, especially my death? Will they say I died, O God? If they don't say I died how can I die? There it is fine and relevant to die, an honor so to speak, interesting as divorce.

What's in my file at the FBI? What's my symbol when they flick me out? Am I a good American or a borderline case? Can I hold my liquor? Have I ever been cleared, and if so, of what?

Dear Fame, I meet you in the damndest places. You smile, you walleyed bitch, but you look over my shoulder for a prearranged signal: something has come up on the other side of the room.

My life, my own, who is writing you on what pale punch cards? Deep-thinking machine, have you got my number?

A hundred oligarchs in identical suits are sitting around a table shaped like a uterus, alphabetizing greatness. I say to myself: all men are great. I would like to cry but have forgotten how. Now I remember: they used to come to me, those journalists with humble pencils. They begged me from their hats: say something big; give us an execution; make bad weather. I failed them badly. I couldn't grow a beard.

I guess I haven't built my ship of death. The word "image" is now in government. The doors are all closing by remote control. But when I meet the almighty Publicity Director, name-dropper of kings, I'll shake his hand and say: once I kissed Fame (mouth like an ass hole) but only for fun. He'll tear up the punch cards and think for a minute.

The Funeral of Poetry

The password of the twentieth century: Communications (as if we had to invent them). Animals and cannibals have communications; birds and bees and even a few human creatures called artists (generally held to be insane). But the bulk of humanity had to invent Communications. The Romans had the best roads in the world, but had nothing to communicate over them except other Romans. Americans have conquered world-time and world-space and chat with the four corners of the earth at breakfast. The entire solar system is in the hands of cartoonists.

I am sitting in the kitchen in Nebraska and watching a shrouded woman amble down the market in Karachi. She is going to get her morning smallpox shot. It's cold and mental love they want. It's the mystic sexuality of Communications. The girl hugs the hi-fi speaker to her belly: it pours into her openings like gravy. Money was love. Power was love. Communications now are love. In the spring Hitler arises. This is the time of trampling.

A man appears at the corner of the street; I prepare myself for hospitality. Man or angel, welcome! But I am afraid and double-lock the door. On the occasion of the death of a political party, I send an epitaph by Western Union. I didn't go to the funeral of poetry. I stayed home and watched it on television.

From
Selected Poems
(1968)

Manhole Covers

The beauty of manhole covers — what of that?
Like medals struck by a great savage khan,
Like Mayan calendar stones, unliftable, indecipherable,
Not like the old electrum, chased and scored,
Mottoed and sculptured to a turn,
But notched and whelked and pocked and smashed
With the great company names
(Gentle Bethlehem, smiling United States).
This rustproof artifact of my street,
Long after roads are melted away will lie
Sidewise in the grave of the iron-old world,
Bitten at the edges,
Strong with its cryptic American,
Its dated beauty.

Calling the Child

From the third floor I beckon to the child
Flying over the grass. As if by chance
My signal catches her and stops her dance
Under the lilac tree;
And I have flung my net at something wild
And brought it down in all its loveliness.
She lifts her eyes to mine reluctantly,
Measuring in my look our twin distress.

Then from the garden she considers me
And, gathering joy, breaks from the closing net
And races off like one who would forget
That there are nets and snares.
But she returns and stands beneath the tree
With great solemnity, with legs apart,
And wags her head at last and makes a start
And starts her humorous marching up the stairs.

Lines for a Unitarian Church

Little church of simple steel I-beams
Set among the squat midwestern houses,
You seem to say and I believe
Body and soul are one,
Man for the world and the world only,
For there is no evil.

Little church without a steeple,
Without the cross, the sword-hilt in the sky,
Without the crazed-glass staining the mystic floor,
You seem to say and I believe
Evil does not exist.

Church of laughter, church of light,
No more the gothic hell, psychotic tower,
Barb-wire star, cruel crescent, mandala,
No more the brothel of the nave, chancre of Guilt
In God's love-nest.

Instead, upon your lawn at church o'clock
A native head sunk in the earth,
A native head chin-deep in the land;
Here the eternal native welcomes you
Welcomes your earliest and best nature,
Welcomes the resurrection into touch.

Little church of friendly steel,
No higher than a human house, as strong,
Beautiful in humid Cincinnati,
Beautiful in the world, inside and out.

Bad Taste, Inc.

I

There is a shop in Paris called Bad Taste
(Le Mauvais Goût) where objets d'art,
Chiefly Victorian, are sold
To wedding couples from the States,
Interior decorators, movie stars,
Rich poets and other sophisticates.
The past peddles the past
To the latest barbarians. Nothing goes to waste:
Yesterday's newspaper, bits of string,
Forgotten comforts, masterpieces.
In Paris nothing goes to waste,
Especially Taste, especially Bad Taste.

II

In America everything goes to waste.
We waste ourselves in the hygienic sun,
We waste the future, burn it to the ground.
Waste in the States is the national industry,
All are consumers — *consume, consume!*
On to the waste pipe, the cloaca americana!

Human Nature

For months and years in a forgotten war
I rode the battle-gray Diesel-stinking ships
Among the brilliantly advertised Pacific Islands,
Coasting the sinister New Guinea Coasts,
All during the killing and hating of a forgotten war.
Now when I drive behind a Diesel-stinking bus
On the way to the university to teach
Stevens and Pound and Mallarmé,
I am homesick for war.

You Call These Poems?

In Hyderabad, city of blinding marble palaces,
White marble university,
A plaything of the Nizam, I read some poetry
By William Carlos Williams, American.
And the educated and the suave Hindus
And the well-dressed Moslems said,
"You call those things poems?
Are those things poems?"

For years I used to write poems myself
That pleased the Moslems and Hindus of culture,
Telling poems in iambic pentameter,
With a masculine inversion in the second foot,
Frozen poems with an ice-pick at the core,
And lots of allusions from other people's books.

Emily Dickinson and Katherine Anne Porter

I

Emily Dickinson's father yanked on the Baptist bell
To call the townspeople to see the sunset,
And the Baptists saw the glory of the sunset
And went home to stained-glass darkness, awfully disappointed
That something really hideous hadn't happened,
Like Hell or the atom bomb.
Old man Dickinson who also fed the sparrows over the snow
With grain from his barn (age seventy-one)
And hid until he saw them peck it up.

"And drove the fastest horse in town."

II

And when Dylan Thomas was introduced
To Katherine Anne Porter in a room full of people,
He stooped and picked her up below the thighs
And raised her to the ceiling like a drink,
And held her straight in the slack-jawed smoke-blue air
Two minutes, five minutes, seven minutes,
While everybody wondered what it meant
To toast the lady with her own body
Or hold her to the light like a plucked flower.

California Winter

It is winter in California, and outside
Is like the interior of a florist shop:
A chilled and moisture-laden crop
Of pink camellias lines the path; and what
Rare roses for a banquet or a bride,
So multitudinous that they seem a glut!

A line of snails crosses the golf-green lawn
From the rosebushes to the ivy bed;
An arsenic compound is distributed
For them. The gardener will rake up the shells
And leave in a corner of the patio
The little mound of empty snails, like skulls.

By noon the fog is burnt off by the sun
And the world's immensest sky opens a page
For the exercises of a future age;
Now jet planes draw straight lines, parabolas,
And x's, which the wind, before they're done,
Erases leisurely or pulls to fuzz.

It is winter in the valley of the vine.
The vineyards crucified on stakes suggest
War cemeteries, but the fruit is pressed,
The redwood vats are brimming in the shed,
And on the sidings stand tank cars of wine,
For which bright juice a billion grapes have bled.

And skiers from the snow line driving home
Descend through almond orchards, olive farms,
Fig tree and palm tree — everything that warms
The imagination of the wintertime.
If the walls were older one would think of Rome:
If the land were stonier one would think of Spain.

But this land grows the oldest living things,
Trees that were young when Pharaohs ruled the world,
Trees whose new leaves are only just unfurled.
Beautiful they are not; they oppress the heart
With gigantism and with immortal wings;
And yet one feels the sumptuousness of this dirt.

It is raining in California, a straight rain
Cleaning the heavy oranges on the bough,
Filling the gardens till the gardens flow,
Shining the olives, tiling the gleaming tile,
Waxing the dark camellia leaves more green,
Flooding the daylong valleys like the Nile.

A Selection
of Poems

(1969–92)

There Was That Roman Poet

There was that Roman poet who fell in love at fifty-odd.
My God, *Venus*, goddess of love, he cried,
Venus, for Christsake, for the love of God,
Don't do that to me!
Don't let me fall in love, a man of my age.
I beg you on my knobby knees, lay off.
Basta! I've had enough — not only that,
NON SUM QUALIS ERAM, Jesus Christ!
How do you know I can get it up!

The laughter of the goddess cool as hell
Pinged like a Cellini shell.
Priceless, she said, showing her teeth, clacking her castanets, stomping her
    feet.
And what has age to do with that, Quintus, she said,
And put that in your Classical Dictionary . . .
And went her way in a wild odor of roses and garlic.

W.H.A.

Without him many of us would have never happened
But would have gone on being Georgians or worse;
We all recall how he galloped into verse
On Skelton's nag and easily reopened

Eighteenth-century prosody like a can of worms,
And there like Alice on a checkerboard
Careened through Marx and Freud and Kierkegaard
Dazzled and dazzling all the ideas and forms,

And camped out in the United States to wrinkle
Like an Indian squaw to await the Nobel Prize
And study savages with paleface eyes
And sit on Oxford Dictionaries and rankle.

God bless this poet who took the honest chances;
God bless the live poets whom his death enhances.

The Old Poet

Coming to the end of his dated poems in the complete edition, knowing what he did not—the date already written, how many weeks were left, the very number of minutes. I read as with a burning-glass. And so many years between the opening page and a man lingering over the final words in a foreign country—after which there is only an index.

That radiance of old poets (those who surrendered power with a smile). In his own city he renames the streets, the ships, the bars. History comes to his hand like a tame pigeon. One of his sentences hangs in the square like the plume of a volcano. Real speech, real life are unwritten. Only these lines have a tendency to remain forever. Cities with poetry remember him. Cities without poetry.

Mozart's Jew

Much as I enjoy your minor immortality, Da Ponte, I marvel where you lie. New Jersey; New York; something like that. My God, Da Ponte, you gave Mozart the words for all that music. And why do you make me uneasy? Because you were a Jew, Emanuele Conegliano? Because you were a Catholic priest, harried from town to town, country to country, for your love affairs? Because you lie and cover up in your book, only to be caught red-handed? What difference does it make. You called yourself a poet, you fraud, but you had guts. Writing three plays for three different composers at once, and one of them Mozart. And his the *Don Giovanni!* Writing twelve hours on end, like a Hollywood hack. And plenty of Tokay on the table (*goût de terroir*) and lots of Seville tobacco, not to mention the sixteen-year-old girl, your mistress during this project. I like you Da Ponte. And finally bounced out of Europe itself, to open a grocery store in New Jersey, that's almost too much. And failing at it, of course. And yet I think you must have been the first to say of Mozart: the greatest composer, past, present and future. That little bit took genius to say. And the Emperor Joseph liked you. And Casanova, jailed for reading Voltaire. All of you Don Giovannis I like, and you especially, Mozart's Jew, Da Ponte.

The Humanities Building

All the bad Bauhaus comes to a head
In this gray slab, this domino, this plinth
Standing among the olives or the old oak trees,
As the case may be, and whatever the clime.
No bells, no murals, no gargoyles,
But rearing like a fort with slits of eyes
Suspicious in the aggregate, its tons
Of concrete, glaciers of no known color,
Gaze down upon us. Saint Thomas More,
Behold the Humanities Building!
                                          On the top floor
Are one and a half professors of Greek,
Kicked upstairs but with the better view,
And two philosophers, and assorted Slavics;
Then stacks of languages coming down,
Mainly the mother tongue and its dissident children
(History has a building all its own)
To the bottom level with its secretaries,
Advisors, blue-green photographic light
Of many precious copying machines
Which only the girls are allowed to operate.
And all is bathed in the cool fluorescence
From top to bottom, justly distributed
Light, Innovation, Progress, Equity;
Though in my cell I hope and pray
Not to be confronted by
A student with a gun or a nervous breakdown,
Or a girl who closes the door as she comes in.

The Old Guard sits in judgment and wears ties,
Eying the New in proletarian drag,
Where the Assistant with one lowered eyelid
Plots against Tenure, dreaming of getting it;

And in the lobby, under the bulletin boards,
The Baudelairean forest of posters
For Transcendental Meditation, Audubon Group,
"The Hunchback of Notre Dame," Scientology,
Arab Students Co-op, "Case of the Curious Bride,"
Two students munch upon a single sandwich.

Crossing Lincoln Park

Dit le corbeau, jamais plus. — *Mallarmé*

Car locked, I started home across the grass,
A kind of island with a stand of oaks
Washed round on all sides by the swish of cars,
To where I lived, a hundred yards in view.
Quarried apartments rose on every hand,
Scoriac Gothic shouldering solid glass
Hemming me in, reflecting a blank sky.
Briefcase and I happily homeward strode
Through ankle-grass, when something at my shoe
Darkly turned over, what I never knew,
For down came the crow and with a sudden blow,
Its great wings beating, slashed at my face
With croak and scream and yellow beak
Screeching me out. I did not stop to think
But leapt and sprinted toward the curb, the bird
Cursing, crisscrossing, driving at my face,
Crashing my shoulders with its filthy wings.
Ugly, omnivorous offal-eating crow,
Bird of ill omen,
Eater of turd and dead fish, get thy beak
From out my heart! My eyeglasses flew off,
I stumbled forward, clutching my briefcase,
Fanning away the bird with naked hand,
Until I reached the street where solid cars
Bumper to bumper blocked my flight,
And still the crow surrounded me and struck
Till I broke through and in the door and up
The elevator to the velvet hall
And to the door and in, where your bright smile
Changed instantly to — "White!" you said.
"Your face whiter than chalk!"

My Father's Funeral

Lurching from gloomy limousines we slip
On the warm baby-blanket of Baltimore snow,
Wet flakes smacking our faces like distraught
Kisses on cheeks, and step upon the green
Carpet of artificial grass which crunches
Underfoot, as if it were eating, and come
To the canopy, a half-shelter which provides
A kind of room to enclose us all, and the hole,
And the camp chairs, and following after,
The scrolly walnut coffin
That has my father in it.

Minutes ago in the noncommittal chapel
I saw his face, not looking himself at all
In that compartment hinged to open and shut,
A vaudeville prop with a small waxen man,
"So cold," the widow said and shied away
In a wide arc of centrifugal motion,
To come again to stand like me beside,
In the flowerless room with electric candelabra.
If there is among our people any heaven,
We are rather ambiguous about it
And tend to ignore the subject.

The rabbi's eulogy is succinct,
Accurate and sincere, and the great prayer
That finishes the speech is simply praise
Of God, the god my father took in stride
When he made us learn Hebrew and shorthand,
Taught us to be superior, as befits
A nation of individual priests.
At my sister's house we neither pray nor cry
Nor sit, but stand and drink and joke,
So that one of the youngsters says
It's more like a cocktail party.

For Dylan's dandy villanelle,
For Sylvia's oath of damnation one reserves
A technical respect. To Miller's Willie
And Lewis's Babbitt I demur.
My father was writing a book on salesmanship
While he was dying; it was his book of poems.
Destined to be unpublished. He hadn't time
To master books but kept the house well stocked
With random volumes, like a ship's library,
Rows and rows of forgotten classics,
Books for the sake of having books.

My father in black knee-socks and high shoes
Holding a whip to whip a top upstreet;
My father the court stenographer,
My father in slouch hat in the Rockies,
My father kissing my mother,
My father kissing his secretary,
In the high-school yearbook captioned Yid,
In synagogue at six in the morning praying
Three hundred and sixty-five days for his mother's rest,
My father at my elbow on the bimah
And presiding over the Sabbath.

In the old forgotten purlieus of the city
A Jewish ghetto in its day, there lie
My father's father, mother and the rest,
Now only a ghetto lost to time,
Ungreen, unwhite, unterraced like the new
Cemetery to which my father goes.
Abaddon, the old place of destruction;
Sheol, a new-made garden of the dead
Under the snow. Shalom be to his life,
Shalom be to his death.

Moving In

I wish you for your birthday as you are,
Inherently happy,
The little girl always shining out of your face
And the woman standing her ground.

Wish you the seldom oceanic earthquake
Which shatters your gaze
Against some previous interior past
And rights you.

Wish you your honesty normal as a tree
Confounding the caws of intellectuals.
When I zip your dress I kiss you on the neck,
A talisman in honor of your pride.

When I hold your head in my hands
It is as of the roundness of Columbus
Thinking the world, "my hands capable of
Designing the earthly sphere."

Your fingers on the piano keys
Or the typewriter keys or on my face
Write identical transcriptions.
Nothing you do is lost in translation.

I am delighted that you loathe Christmas.
I feel the same way about Communism.
Let us live in the best possible house,
Selfish and true.

May the Verdi *Requiem* continue to knock you out
As it does me; fashionable protest art
Continue to infuriate your heart
And make you spill your drink.

Now ideology has had its day
Nothing is more important than your birthday.
Let us have a solid roof over our head
And bless one another.

A Curiosity

Tiny bees come to see what I am,
Lying in the sun at summer's end,
Writing a poem on a reclining chair.
A butterfly approaches and retreats;
Flies bang into my body by mistake,
And tinier things I can't identify;
And now and then a slow gigantic wasp
Rows on its stately voyage to the fence.
The trees are still too little to have birds;
Besides, the neighbors all have special cats
Bred for their oddity or arrogance.
A dragonfly sips at a lemon twig
After a helicopter landing. It
Appears that I am a curiosity
In my own backyard.
The dog of doubtful breed
Sleeps on the carpet of the sod,
And a bee necks with a rose.

The Piano Tuner's Wife

That note comes clear, like water running clear,
Then the next higher note, and up and up
And more and more, with now and then a chord,
The highest notes like tapping a tile with a hammer,
Now and again an arpeggio, a theme,
As if the keyboard spoke to the one key,
Saying, No interval is exactly true,
And the note whines slightly and then truly sings.

She sits on the sofa reading a book she has brought,
A ray of sunlight on her white hair.
She is here because he is blind. She drives.
It is almost a platitude to say
That she leads him from piano to piano.

And this continues for about an hour,
Building bridges from both sides of the void,
Coasting the chasms of the harmonies.

And in conclusion,
When there is no more audible dissent,
He plays his comprehensive keyboard song,
The loud proud paradigm,
The one work of art without content.

At Auden's Grave

From Vienna it's picture postcard all the way.
Where else on earth is such a land at ease!
The fat farms glistening, the polished pigs,
Each carven window box disgorging red
Geraniums, pencil pines and chestnut trees,
The gaily painted tractor rigs,
Steeples with onion domes that seem to say
Grüss Gott, come lie here in our flowerbed.

How many times did Auden take this train
Till that bright autumn day when he was borne
Back in a baggage car after his last
Recital, back to his Horatian house,
His cave of making, now the mask outworn,
The geographical visage consummated,
Back to the village, home to the country man
Without a country, home to the urban bard
Without a city he could call his own.

But suddenly a startling word
Leaps from the signpost of the country lane,
It's AUDENSTRASSE —
The poet becomes a street, the street a poet,
English with German music mated.

Here will arrive no pilgrim mob
As in Westminster Abbey, where his name
Is chiseled next to Eliot's. The sole cab
Has never heard of Auden, has to ask
Gasthaus directions, but we find him there
Ten yards away and settled with his slab,
The bracketed dates, the modest designation,
His plot planted to suffocation
In the country style of *horror vacui*.

Close by, a granite soldier stands
Bareheaded, bowed, without a gun,
Wearing his empty cartridge belt,
A blunt reminder of the First World War,
Signed *Unseren Helden* for those villagers
Who never returned and lay somewhere in France
Entre deux guerres before the next
World War should be begun
By the ultimate twentieth century hun.

Far from his foggy isle
The poet rests in self-exile.
Earth of the great composers of the wordless art
Enshrouds this master of the English tune
Not many miles from where Beethoven scrawled his will
When he could no longer hear the trill
Of the little yellow-hammer, nor the titanic storm.
In such a place Dame Kind
Released the intellectual minstrel's form.

Across the *Audenstrasse* from the grave
A bee drops from the chestnut, sips the beer,
Brings back his image to me, on a day
I bought him a tin collapsible cup to sip
His whiskey from, on some Iowa train,
Knowing his dread of that vertiginous plain.
Now all is comfy in his delectable cave.
I scatter the bee and greet him with my lip.

Whatever commentators come to say —
That life was not your bag — Edwardian —
Misogynist — Greenwich Villager —
Drifter — coward — traitorous clerk — or you,
In your own language, genteel anti-Jew —
I come to bless this plot where you are lain,
Poet who made poetry whole again.

Sandwiched between two families Auden lies,
At last one of the locals, over his grave
A cross, a battle monument, and a name
History will polish to a shine.
Down in the valley hums the Autobahn,
Up here the poet lies sleeping in a vale
That has no exits. All the same,
Right on target and just in time
A NATO fighter rips open the skies
Straight over Auden's domus and is gone.

The Old Horsefly

Unseasonable weather, says the commentator,
Seventy in Manhattan in December.
Flu bugs as big as pigeons, I advise.

I saw a bee buzzing a sidewalk florist
On Broadway under a wall of Christmas trees.

Eleven floors up in the too-warm living room
A horsefly dashes window to wall and back,
A horsefly in December in Manhattan,
Off-course like those venturesome seagulls
Flying between two rivers and two parks
When the wind is right.
                    I get the flyswatter.

No entomologist, I decide
This is an old horsefly. I'll let it go,
Or is it a gadfly from the hotel row
Where carriage horses from another world
Still nod and stomp and swish their horsehair tails?

Its flight is frantic but I know that flies
That find their way in windows never find
The exit. I watch it speeding to and fro,
Disappearing, exploring other rooms
Till tired it lights on a white-painted door.

Biped approaches, raises his wand, then strikes.
Did I get it? I feel a pang — of what?

Tennyson

Like many of us he was rather disgusting
With his deliberate dirtiness, his myopia, his smell,
His undying enmity for unfavorable reviewers,
His stinginess, his coy greed for titles, money and gowns,
His contempt for Cockneys and Americans,
Sallow, greasy, handsome, the Ur-Victorian.
Stupid, as Auden called him.

And yet, one of the great songsters of the English word,
Though we still say, a century beyond,
With qualifications.
                    And modern!
A family riddled with drugs, alcohol and insanity,
His major themes all givens or hand-me-downs,
The omnium-gatherum of *In Memoriam*
For beloved Arthur, the high-school *Idylls*,
The triumph of faulknerian *Maud*
(Though only Browning could call it great);

Yanking his son out of Cambridge to be his biographer,
The slavey wife he truly cherished,
His fear of Darwin, his desperation for everlastingness;

Beautiful tedious Alfred, nicotine drooling from his
                    meerschaum pipe,
Which he invited guests to suck,
Long-lived, the very image of the English Poet
Whose songs still break out tears in the generations,
Whose prosody for practitioners still astounds,
Who crafted his life and letters like a watch.

Whitman

Like Queen Victoria, he used the regal *we*,
Meaning the disciples of *Leaves of Grass*,
The American Bible they literally believed;
Sat by the hour to photographers,
The Open Shirt frontispiece,
The Good Gray, the Jesus, the Laughing Philosopher,
The Old Poet in the crumpled highcrown hat
Gazing in rapture at the butterfly
        Perched upon his forefinger
(It turns out was a cardboard butterfly);
To Tennyson the greatest of his time,
Inviting Walt to sail to the Isle of Wight;
Our first and probably our only guru,
Whose opinion of niggers (his designation) was low,
But worshipped Lincoln, to whom he scribed
        His second greatest song;
Who opened the Closet but wouldn't come out;
Who lived in a kind of luxurious poverty,
Housekeeper, male nurse, amanuensis, carriage,
        On the bounty of admirers,
Adored as Gandhi or a Dr. Schweitzer,
Visited by Oscar Wilde and English titles,
        In Camden, New Jersey;
Two hundred pounds of genius and hype,
Nature-mystic who designed his tomb
Solid as an Egyptian pyramid,
American to the soles of his boots,
Outspoken as Christ or Madame Blavatsky,
Messiah, Muse of the Modern, Mother!

Future-Present

Remember the old days when the luxury liners
                in narrow Manhattan
appeared piecemeal in segments at the end of east-west
                streets,
a black-and-white section of portholes and stripes of decks
and slowly the majesty of the great red funnel,
even the olympian basso of its homing horn?
It would take a full half hour to go past,
as if in no hurry to pass into history.

But look there at the top pane of the window!
A burnished skyliner elegantly moving north,
as proud as leviathan above the suffering Hudson,
past the unfinished cathedral, over Grant's tomb,
into the blue-gray morning of the future-present.

July 7, 1978

for Sophie

You marked the day
that, sitting in a tired chair,
gazing toward the exhausted light
white and silent as the telephone
it came to you, that ray,

why scamp it, that annunciation
hundreds of masters tried to paint,
the flêche d'amour that marks the way
from the quotidian penitentiary
to your epiphany.

Jacob Boehme saw it in a ray
that struck a pewter pot,
Whitman saw it where he lay
outstretched on the uncut hair of graves.
It came to you
wholly unbidden from your inner day.

Acknowledgments

To find oneself "selected" and published without moving a finger is a foretaste of an afterlife — a quasi-illicit joy. This I owe to Stanley Kunitz, who first thought of it and then, with David Ignatow, saw it through to completion, also inspiring the late M. L. Rosenthal to write the excellent introduction. Arranging for this publication is only the latest instance of Robert Phillips's rare, supportive friendship over the years.

—K.S.

Karl Shapiro (b. 1913) is one of the most distinguished poets of America's Middle Generation, the generation of Lowell, Schwartz, Berryman, Roethke, and Bishop. Shapiro's second poetry collection, *V-Letter and Other Poems*, was awarded the Pulitzer Prize in 1945. In 1946 he was appointed Consultant in Poetry at the Library of Congress, the position now called U.S. Poet Laureate. From 1950 to 1956 he was editor of *Poetry: A Magazine of Verse*, and from 1956 to 1966 he edited *Prairie Schooner*. He was awarded the Bollingen Prize in Poetry in 1969. He has taught at Johns Hopkins University, the University of Nebraska, the University of Illinois at Chicago, and the University of California at Davis, from which he retired. He is a member of the American Academy of Arts and Letters and lives in Manhattan with his wife, the translator Sophie Wilkins.

Illinois Poetry Series
Laurence Lieberman, Editor

History Is Your Own Heartbeat
Michael S. Harper (1971)

The Foreclosure
Richard Emil Braun (1972)

The Scrawny Sonnets and Other
Narratives
Robert Bagg (1973)

The Creation Frame
Phyllis Thompson (1973)

To All Appearances: Poems New and
Selected
Josephine Miles (1974)

The Black Hawk Songs
Michael Borich (1975)

Nightmare Begins Responsibility
Michael S. Harper (1975)

The Wichita Poems
Michael Van Walleghen (1975)

Images of Kin: New and Selected
Poems
Michael S. Harper (1977)

Poems of the Two Worlds
Frederick Morgan (1977)

Cumberland Station
Dave Smith (1977)

Tracking
Virginia R. Terris (1977)

Riversongs
Michael Anania (1978)

On Earth as It Is
Dan Masterson (1978)

Coming to Terms
Josephine Miles (1979)

Death Mother and Other Poems
Frederick Morgan (1979)

Goshawk, Antelope
Dave Smith (1979)

Local Men
James Whitehead (1979)

Searching the Drowned Man
Sydney Lea (1980)

With Akhmatova at the Black Gates
Stephen Berg (1981)

Dream Flights
Dave Smith (1981)

More Trouble with the Obvious
Michael Van Walleghen (1981)

The American Book of the Dead
Jim Barnes (1982)

The Floating Candles
Sydney Lea (1982)

Northbook
Frederick Morgan (1982)

Collected Poems, 1930–83
Josephine Miles (1983)

The River Painter
Emily Grosholz (1984)

Healing Song for the Inner Ear
Michael S. Harper (1984)

The Passion of the Right-Angled Man
T. R. Hummer (1984)

Dear John, Dear Coltrane
Michael S. Harper (1985)

Poems from the Sangamon
John Knoepfle (1985)

In It
Stephen Berg (1986)

The Ghosts of Who We Were
Phyllis Thompson (1986)

Moon in a Mason Jar
Robert Wrigley (1986)

Lower-Class Heresy
T. R. Hummer (1987)

Poems: New and Selected
Frederick Morgan (1987)

Furnace Harbor: A Rhapsody of the
North Country
Philip D. Church (1988)

Bad Girl, with Hawk
Nance Van Winckel (1988)

Blue Tango
Michael Van Walleghen (1989)

Eden
Dennis Schmitz (1989)

Waiting for Poppa at the Smithtown Diner
Peter Serchuk (1990)

Great Blue
Brendan Galvin (1990)

What My Father Believed
Robert Wrigley (1991)

Something Grazes Our Hair
S. J. Marks (1991)

Walking the Blind Dog
G. E. Murray (1992)

The Sawdust War
Jim Barnes (1992)

The God of Indeterminacy
Sandra McPherson (1993)

Off-Season at the Edge of the World
Debora Greger (1994)

Counting the Black Angels
Len Roberts (1994)

Oblivion
Stephen Berg (1995)

To Us, All Flowers Are Roses
Lorna Goodison (1995)

Honorable Amendments
Michael S. Harper (1995)

Points of Departure
Miller Williams (1995)

Dance Script with Electric Ballerina
Alice Fulton (reissue, 1996)

To the Bone: New and Selected Poems
Sydney Lea (1996)

Floating on Solitude
Dave Smith (3-volume reissue, 1996)

Bruised Paradise
Kevin Stein (1996)

Walt Whitman Bathing
David Wagoner (1996)

Rough Cut
Thomas Swiss (1997)

Paris
Jim Barnes (1997)

The Ways We Touch
Miller Williams (1997)

The Rooster Mask
Henry Hart (1998)

The Trouble-Making Finch
Len Roberts (1998)

National Poetry Series

Eroding Witness
Nathaniel Mackey (1985)
Selected by Michael S. Harper

Palladium
Alice Fulton (1986)
Selected by Mark Strand

Cities in Motion
Sylvia Moss (1987)
Selected by Derek Walcott

The Hand of God and a Few Bright Flowers
William Olsen (1988)
Selected by David Wagoner

The Great Bird of Love
Paul Zimmer (1989)
Selected by William Stafford

Stubborn
Roland Flint (1990)
Selected by Dave Smith

The Surface
Laura Mullen (1991)
Selected by C. K. Williams

The Dig
Lynn Emanuel (1992)
Selected by Gerald Stern

My Alexandria
Mark Doty (1993)
Selected by Philip Levine

The High Road to Taos
Martin Edmunds (1994)
Selected by Donald Hall

Theater of Animals
Samn Stockwell (1995)
Selected by Louise Glück

The Broken World
Marcus Cafagña (1996)
Selected by Yusef Komunyakaa

Nine Skies
A. V. Christie (1997)
Selected by Sandra McPherson

Other Poetry Volumes

Local Men and *Domains*
James Whitehead (1987)

Her Soul beneath the Bone: Women's
Poetry on Breast Cancer
Edited by Leatrice Lifshitz (1988)

Days from a Dream Almanac
Dennis Tedlock (1990)

Working Classics: Poems on
Industrial Life
*Edited by Peter Oresick and
Nicholas Coles* (1990)

Hummers, Knucklers, and Slow
Curves: Contemporary Baseball
Poems
Edited by Don Johnson (1991)

The Double Reckoning of Christopher
Columbus
Barbara Helfgott Hyett (1992)

Selected Poems
Jean Garrigue (1992)

New and Selected Poems, 1962–92
Laurence Lieberman (1993)

The Dig and *Hotel Fiesta*
Lynn Emanuel (1994)

For a Living: The Poetry of Work
*Edited by Nicholas Coles and
Peter Oresick* (1995)

The Tracks We Leave: Poems on
Endangered Wildlife of North
America
Barbara Helfgott Hyett (1996)

Peasants Wake for Fellini's *Casanova*
and Other Poems
*Andrea Zanzotto; edited and translated
by John P. Welle and Ruth Feldman;
drawings by Federico Fellini and
Augusto Murer* (1997)

Moon in a Mason Jar and *What My
Father Believed*
Robert Wrigley (1997)

The Wild Card: Selected Poems, Early
and Late
*Karl Shapiro; edited by Stanley Kunitz
and David Ignatow* (1998)